ENTERPRISE EXCELLENCE | SERIES

SUSTAINING LEAN

Case Studies in TRANSFORMING CULTURE

Association for Manufacturing Excellence
(AME)

CRC Press
Taylor & Francis Group
Boca Raton   London   New York

CRC Press is an imprint of the
Taylor & Francis Group, an **informa** business

A PRODUCTIVITY PRESS BOOK

AME Association for
Manufacturing Excellence
Enterprise excellence through shared learning

Productivity Press
Taylor & Francis Group
270 Madison Avenue
New York, NY 10016

© 2009 by Association for Manufacturing Excellence
Productivity Press is an imprint of Taylor & Francis Group, an Informa business

No claim to original U.S. Government works
Printed in the United States of America on acid-free paper
10 9 8 7 6 5 4 3 2 1

International Standard Book Number-13: 978-1-4200-8379-8 (Softcover)

Library of Congress Cataloging-in-Publication Data

Sustaining lean : case studies in transforming culture / Association for Manufacturing Excellence.
    p. cm. -- (Enterprise excellence series ; 3)
    ISBN 978-1-4200-8379-8 (alk. paper)
    1. Organizational effectiveness--Case studies. 2. Organizational change--Case studies. 3. Corporate culture--Case studies. I. Association for Manufacturing Excellence (U.S.)

HD58.9.S87 2009
658.4'012--dc22   2008030942

Visit the Taylor & Francis Web site at
http://www.taylorandfrancis.com

and the Productivity Press Web site at
http://www.productivitypress.com

ENTERPRISE EXCELLENCE SERIES

SUSTAINING

HD 62.15 AME

ENTERPRISE EXCELLENCE | SERIES

Series Mission

To share new ideas and examples of excellence through case studies and other reports from all types of organizations, and to show how both leading-edge and proven improvement methods can be applied to a range of operations and industries.

Contents

Series Mission

To share new ideas and examples of excellence through case studies and other reports from all types of organizations, and to show how both leading-edge and proven improvement methods can be applied to a range of operations and industries.

Introduction

One of the most widely recognized challenges facing companies adopting a lean strategy is how to sustain initial momentum and develop a corporate culture with a built-in, ongoing commitment to that strategy. The chapters in this book provide some insights as to how that can be achieved.

These chapters were originally published as articles in the well-regarded magazine *Target*, published by the Association for Manufacturing Excellence. Most of the articles chosen for this collection are case studies; a few more broadly discuss the issues involved in long-term cultural transformation.

In Chapter One, David Mann, Ph.D., author of the book *Creating a Lean Culture: Tools to Sustain Lean Conversions*, discusses just what it means to have a lean culture. He explains the importance of the lean conversion of management systems, as well as production processes, and he describes the need to achieve that conversion through the proper sequence of steps, as well as what questions to ask.

In a similar vein, Chapter Two talks about the "working culture gap" between a typical non-lean organization with a structured flow of operations and an organization that is habitually learning. The focus in this chapter is on leadership, and how leaders must understand and support process excellence, encourage a thinking culture, set strategic direction and create the proper structure.

A case study of an organization that works to achieve all this is the subject of Chapter Three – specifically, Hewlett-Packard America's Software Manufacturing division. Learn in this chapter how the division's employees, led by committed leaders, use training, tools and well-defined goals to sustain their culture.

Batesville Casket Company, the focus of Chapter Four, is also a company that works hard to sustain its culture. This chapter describes how that culture is defined as Daily Continuous Improvement, as well as the company's very strong focus on listening to the voice of the customer.

At Deceuninck North America, the company described in Chapter Five, a culture of continuous improvement is based on a foundation of 5S. While 5S is often viewed as simply one lean tool, the cultural changes and work habits it helps establish can have far-reaching effects in bringing about cultural transformation.

A team-centered approach is at the heart of continuous improvement at General Dynamics Advanced Information Systems, explained in Chapter Six. Key elements include permanent factory teams, temporary kaizen teams, and strong communication among all teams and all employees.

How a struggling company in a declining market turned itself around is the story told in Chapter Seven. Hickory Chair Company, through strong and dedicated leadership as well as a new culture of empowered employees, avoided traveling the outsourcing route chosen by many in its industry, managing not only to maintain U.S. operations but to do so profitably.

At M2 Global, the focus of Chapter Eight, new business demands prompted the company to pursue a multi-pronged effort to redefine itself. That effort included tapping into the knowledge and expertise of the workforce, finding a better manufacturing philosophy, and embracing an adaptation of quality function deployment.

A fully engaged HR department can be valuable in sustaining lean culture, or so argue Dr. Monica Tracey and Jamie Flinchbaugh in Chapter Nine. Basing their comments about research on lean transformations, they offer specific recommendations to HR managers regarding their role in these transformations.

Whether you are in the early stages of building a lean culture or far along the journey, you face the challenge of sustaining that effort. The chapters in this book can be a valuable resource in meeting that challenge.

1

The Case for Lean Culture: Sustain the gains from your lean conversion

David Mann, Ph.D.

IN BRIEF

Becoming a lean organization means transforming not just production processes, but management as well. A lean management system is an integral element of the lean process, critical to sustaining gains. It is important to understand what lean culture is and what issues must be addressed or obstacles overcome to create that culture.

There's a missing link in most descriptions of lean manufacturing. It's lean culture, and a lean management system to go with it. Management practices for lean and the lean culture that grows from them are like many other aspects of lean: easy to grasp but difficult to consistently execute. This article provides a framework to understand three related topics: the nature of lean and mass production cultures, how lean management practices differ from those in mass production, and the nature of the task in changing from mass to lean culture.

"Culture" and "management system" are used interchangeably in this article. The lean management system consists of the discipline, daily practices, and tools needed to sustain and extend lean implementations. Lean culture grows from these practices when the practices become habitual, a way of thinking or mindset. So, don't focus on "culture" as a target. Focus instead on behavior, on habits and practices, extinguishing the old and reinforcing the new. As you prepare to do this, be aware that the task is formidable. The lion's share of what it takes to make lean conversions long-running success stories is the change in management systems from mass to lean.

First, consider lean production. Lean manufacturing is an idea whose time has come. Manufacturers the world over have recognized the advantages in leadtime, productivity, quality, and cost enjoyed by lean competitors in industry after industry. One of the attractive features of lean is that it's so easy to understand. Customer focus, value stream organization, standardized work, flow, pull, and continuous improvement are readily grasped.

Second, lean is typically not capital intensive; it relies on simple, single-purpose equipment with minimal automation. Lean scheduling systems are equally simple and inexpensive, rarely requiring much if anything in the way of incremental IT investment. Finally, lean layouts and material flows are relatively straightforward to design and implement whether through redesign of entire value streams or more narrowly-focused kaizen events.

PARALLEL IMPLEMENTATIONS

So, lean production confers many advantages. It is easily grasped, requires minimal capital for equipment and systems support, and is relatively straightforward to implement. Yet, the experience of many — indeed, most — companies that have attempted to convert to lean production has been failure and retreat. This is one of the paradoxes of lean. It seems so easy, yet success is so difficult!

What is it about lean that makes successful implementation so rare as to be newsworthy? Something, some crucial ingredient, must be missing from the standard list of steps in lean conversions. The missing link is this: a parallel lean conversion effort, that is, one that converts management systems from mass production to lean.

CHANGING FROM WHAT, TO WHAT?

The physical changes in a lean conversion are easy to see: Equipment gets rearranged, inventory is reduced and deployed in new ways, there are notable changes in material supply, production scheduling, and standard-ized methods. The change in management systems is not so obvious. An orienting question about the lean management system might be: Change *from* what, *to* what?

FROM: CONVENTIONAL MASS PRODUCTION

Think about management in a conventional mass production operation. First and foremost, the focus is on results, on hitting the numbers: Did we meet the schedule for this day or this week? How many defective units were caught by quality inspections? Did we hit our targets for material cost and production labor? Managers in conventional systems track key indicators like these through monitoring and analysis of reports that summarize the previous period's (day, week, or month) data.

Managers attend many meetings to review production status and trouble-shoot problems. These meetings typically revolve around computer-gener-ated reports that line managers and support group specialists pore over in conference rooms. Disagreements are common about which departments' reports to believe. (These disagreements can sometimes be resolved only by doing actual cycle counts or other research on the production floor!) The focus is usually retrospective, looking at what happened last reporting period, determining who or what messed up, and deciding how to recover. With more sophisticated IT systems, these data are accessible more or less in "real" time. Looking at a computer monitor, managers can see a numer-ical or even graphic reflection of the state of their production process. This seems like an improvement, and often can be — provided one can sift through all the available data to identify the critical numbers to watch.

FROM: DO WHATEVER IT TAKES!

When problems arise that threaten schedule completion, the common practice is "do whatever it takes" to meet the schedule. Expedite internal parts, pressure suppliers, airfreight late materials, put on more people, pressure the inspectors, reorder missing parts with a fudge factor to make sure you get the few good ones you need, authorize overtime. Just meet the schedule! Tomorrow or next week, it's a new day with a new schedule and new challenges. Things that went wrong yesterday are typically dropped in the press to meet today's demands. After all, today's schedule must be met!

In fact, most manufacturing managers have learned how to be successful in this kind of system. They know the workarounds and tricks to ensure success in an uncertain environment where the bottom might fall out in one of several areas on any given day. The tricks of the trade include "secret" stashes of extra material, people, and even equipment to be called on in time of need.[1] Never mind that all this is costly in the long run. In the short run, results are what matter and the numbers don't lie; you either met the schedule or you didn't.

TO: LEAN PRODUCTION AND LEAN MANAGEMENT

In lean systems the results certainly matter but the approach to achieving them differs sharply from conventional management methods. The difference in a lean management system is the addition of a focus on process *as well* as a focus on results. The premise is this: Start by designing a *process* to produce specific results. If you've done a good job of designing the process and you maintain it, you'll get the specified results. In concept, this is simply a matter of maintaining production at takt time. If you do, you meet demand. As you make improvements in the process, you should expect improved results.

TO: LEAN PROCESSES NEED LEAN MANAGEMENT

A critical point is to think about the lean management system as an integral element of the lean process. Here's why. If the process was a perfect system, it would always run as designed and always produce consistent results. A real-world system requires periodic maintenance and occasional intervention and repair to continue producing results. The more complex the system, especially the more automated it is, the more maintenance and repair it requires. It may not seem like this should be true, but it is. A more reliable and flexible solution usually is to rely less on automation and more on people and simpler equipment.

Relying on people brings its own set of issues. People require all sorts of "maintenance" and attention. Left to their own devices, people are prone to introduce all kinds of "mischief," that is, variation in the system that can take things far afield from the original design. If anything, lean production is more vulnerable to these effects than mass production because of the tight interdependence and reliance on precise execution in lean designs. That's why discipline is such an important factor in lean processes. Without a high degree of discipline in a lean process, chaos ensues in short order. That's where the lean management system comes in.

TO: PROCESS FOCUS PRODUCES RESULTS

Putting it plainly, if you want a process to produce the results it was designed for, you have to pay attention to it. One of the first rules of process focus in lean production is regularly seeing the process operating *with your own eyes*. The closer your position is to the production floor (value stream manager, department supervisor, team leader as opposed to plant manager, manufacturing director, or VP), the more time you should spend watching the process, verifying execution consistent with design, and intervening when you observe nonstandard or abnormal conditions. Production team leaders should spend virtually *all* of their time training operators in the process, monitoring the process, or improving it. Taking time to monitor the production process applies all the way up the chain of command, though with decreasing frequency and duration. That's why lean manufacturing executives meet with their plant managers out on the production floor, to spot-verify that processes are defined, are visually documented and controlled, and are being followed. It also allows executives to verify plant managers know what's going on with their lean processes. Meetings and discussion of reports in conference rooms become secondary activities in management reviews.

Another way of thinking about this, and another paradox in lean management, is that lean managers are so focused on results that they can't afford to take their eyes off the process they rely on to produce their results. Looking at what happened yesterday is way too late to do anything about yesterday's results. On the other hand, looking at what happened last hour, last pitch, or even better, last takt cycle gives the chance to recover from an abnormal or nonstandard condition. But that's only true if trained eyes (like a team leader's) are there to see the abnormality and the pertinent processes are well defined, clearly documented, operating in a stable environment, and resources are available to respond in *real* real time. That is, someone is available to respond *right now!*

Further, this means focusing on the process as it operates from beginning to end, not only at the finished component or finished goods end. That's why lean designs require so many team leaders, to spot problems in upstream intermediate or sub-process areas and to respond right away to prevent or minimize missing takt at the outlet end of the process. An integral part of the lean management system is having the appropriate number of team leaders on the floor to focus on the process. It requires a leap of faith not to scrimp on this crucial part of the system; having enough leaders available to monitor the process, react to problems, and work toward root cause solutions is an investment that pays off in business results. But at first, and from a conventional perspective, team leaders just look like more overhead.

TO: PROCESS STANDARDS AND MEASURES

Unlike managing in a results-focused system, process focus implies frequent measurement against expected intermediate outcomes. As necessary, interventions can be started before the end results are affected. A corollary of frequent measurement at multiple intermediate steps in a lean process is that data are readily available to aid quick diagnosis of problems, spur immediate remedial action, and eventually eliminate root causes of problems. This is one aspect of continuous improvement. Rather than waiting for problems to develop, you're constantly monitoring for early signs of developing troubles, and are primed to take quick action to eliminate the causes of problems. Contrast this approach with the conventional mass production culture in which most supervisors expect various unpredictable problems and have earned their spurs by being able to work around them to get out the day's schedule.

A new management system is called for in lean conversions because lean processes are much more tightly interdependent than conventional systems and are designed not to have the extras stashed away to use in a pinch to bail out conventional systems. Even so, things go wrong in lean systems just as they do in mass systems. By design there's little unaccounted-for slack in the system to fall back on in a lean process. Because of that, lean processes require far more attention to disciplined, cycle-by-cycle operation to be sure the process stays in a stable state. Otherwise, the process will fail to hit its goals and fail to deliver the business results so important in any kind of production system. Paradoxically then, "simpler" lean systems in many ways require more maintenance than conventional systems. That's why they require a specific management system to sustain them.

WHAT IS LEAN CULTURE?

For our purposes, we can define culture in a work organization as the sum of many individuals' habits related to the work in the organization. A related way to think of culture is that it's the knowledge of how things are done that an adult needs to stay out of trouble as a member of a group. One of the interesting things about culture is that for group members, culture is invisible. It's the things that are "given," or "the way we do things around here." It's typical not to question this kind of thing, or even to realize there are alternatives to it. Yet, it's easily possible to "see" work culture in a production environment by asking basic questions about common practices, such as these:

1. What are inventory practices around here?
2. How often does management look at the status of production here?
3. Who's involved in process improvement activities in this area?

Asking these questions would reveal some of the distinctions between the cultures in conventional and lean production environments.

Visible Attributes of Culture in Mass and Lean Production

Cultural Attribute	Mass Production Culture	Lean Production Culture
Inventory practices:	Managed by computer system	Managed Visually
	Ordered by forecast	Ordered based on actual use
	Stored in warehouse areas or automated storage and retrieval facilities	Stored in flow racks or grids addressed by part number
	Held in bulk containers	Held in point-of-use containers; container quantity + number of containers specified per address
	Moved by lift truck	Deliveries by hand cart or tugger
	Many hours' worth or more per deliver	Precise quantities (often < an hour's worth) delivered to point of use
	Delivered by the skid or tub by hi-lo	Deliveries by hand cart or tugger
Production status:	Checked at end of shift, beginning of next shift, or end of week	Checked by a team of leaders several times an hour
	Checked by supervisor, higher level managers	Checked by supervisors four or more times a shift
		Checked by superintendents once or twice during the shift
		Updated for all involved in a sequence of brief daily reviews of the previous day's performance
Process improvement:	Made by technical project teams	Can and routinely are initiated by anybody, including operators
	Changes must be specifically "chartered"	Regular, structured vehicles encourage everyone from the floor on up to suggest improvements and perhaps get involved in implementation
	No changes between "official" projects	Improvement goes on more or less all the time, continuously

FIGURE 1.1

The examples in Figure 1.1 give a partial picture of the "everyday-ness" of culture. It's made up of myriad habits and practices that make it possible for people to go through their work day without having constantly to think about who, what, where, when, how, and so on. Culture allows us to operate more or less on autopilot during the workday. By the same token, a distinct culture also makes it easy to identify counter-cultural behaviors, practices, or events.

CULTURAL INERTIA

One implication of culture as a collection of habits and practices is that it has incredible inertia and momentum going for it. Cultural inertia is like a body in motion, tending to stay in motion in the same direction unless acted on by an external force.

Conventional mass production systems include a culture. So do lean production systems. When you change the physical arrangements from mass to lean, however, the culture does not change from mass to lean unless specific action is taken to replace one management system with another. That's the "parallel" lean implementation noted earlier, implementing the lean management system.

Conventional habits and practices live on even if the layout, material, and information flows have changed. For example, operators whose area switched from MRP (Material Requirements Planning) schedules to pull signals were quite inventive figuring out how to get access to a schedule they then followed regardless of the pull signals. In this example, the fabrication operators regularly produced according to the discarded schedule they retrieved every day from a trashcan near the dispatch office until they were found out and the schedule paperwork was shredded. Another common occurrence is for operators in newly-converted flow lines transformed from batch build to go right on building. When the line fills up, it's typical to see the overproduction stacked on the floor or conveyors, overflowing containers, etc.[2]

NEW SETTINGS, OLD HABITS

Similarly, it's typical to see supervisors and team leaders in a newly rearranged area rushing off here and there to chase parts or jump onto the line to run production. In some cases, it's nearly impossible to convince supervisors or team leaders to make the hourly entries on production tracking charts because they're "too busy" to get to this task. Then, once the tracking charts are actually filled out, it's not unusual to see them simply pile up on (or under) a supervisor's desk with no attention at all to the interruptions documented on the charts. If the schedule has been met, there's no interest in what's on that "paperwork." And if the schedule hasn't been met, there's "real work" to be done; no time to waste with these records of interruption! That won't get the schedule out today, and in the old — and ingrained — culture, that's all that counts.

In conventional mass production, it's seen as important to be busy doing something directly physically linked to production. Waiting for a production instruction card to arrive before starting to produce simply seems wrong. Standing and waiting for the next piece to come down a progressive build line is definitely counter-cultural in the mass production world. In such an environment, these interruptions in the rhythm of production are not considered to be valuable diagnostic information signaling an abnormal condition in the production system, that's for sure! Relying on the reduced inventory of parts called for in a pull system seems sure to lead to stock-outs down the line. There's no perceived value in recording data that documents the operation of the process. Action is what counts, and if it's based on gut feel and experience, it must be right because "that's the way we get things done around here."

These are only a few habits of thought, interpretation, and action that people absorb as part of the culture in a mass production environment. They are at clear variance with the kinds of habits and daily practices necessary for the precise and disciplined execution lean systems need in order to meet their promise for productivity, quality, and ongoing improvement. A few of the ways in which mass and lean cultures differ are shown in Figure 1.2. Many mass production cultural practices are strikingly tied to longstanding ways of relating to others at work while many lean practices are related to disciplined adherence to defined processes. (See the accompanying box, "A Note on Attitudes.")

CHANGING CULTURES: THE NATURE OF THE TASK

We usually refer to changing habits with the word "break," as in, "That's a hard habit to break." Similarly, many talk about "kicking" habits. In each case, these words imply that changing habits is an event, a discontinuous step-change from one state to another which, once accomplished is a one-time event that's over and done with, and no going back.

Differences in Habits and Practices Between
Mass Production and Lean Production Cultures

Mass Production: Personality Focused Work Practices	Lean Production: Process-Focused Work Practices
Independent	Interdependent, closely linked
Self-paced work and breaks	Paced by process, time as a discipline
Leave me alone	I work as part of a team
I get my own parts and supplies	In- and out-cycle work are separated and standardized
We do whatever it takes to get the job done	There's a defined process for pretty much everything; following the process
I define my own methods	Methods are standardized
Results are the focus; do whatever it takes	Process focus is the path to consistent results
Improvement is someone else's job; it's not my responsibility	Improvement is the job of everyone
Maintenance takes care of the equipment when it breaks; it's not my responsibility	Taking care of the equipment to minimize unplanned downtime is routine
Managed by the pay or bonus system	Managed by performance to expectations

FIGURE 1.2

Many habits that come to mind are personal and physical in nature. Smoking, nail biting, various forms of fidgeting — jingling pocket change, fiddling with an ID badge, a pen, or glasses, etc. At some level, each habit provides some form of comfort. We don't think of our work habits so much because many of them are part of the particular culture at work, and that's effectively invisible. Nevertheless, these habits arise because they bring some form of comfort, too. In a conversion to lean production, some of these habits will be a hindrance and some will be a help.

Here are some examples of management habits in conventional mass production operations:

- Keep a quantity of extra material stashed away at all times; you might need it.
- Take time to listen to what people want to tell you.
- Always maintain a minimum ten percent surplus labor and plenty of WIP; something could go wrong.
- Speak to everybody in the department every day.

A NOTE ON ATTITUDES

Many lean conversions include a change management program focused on employees' attitudes toward the change. That's because leaders anticipate substantial resistance to the new, leaner ways of working and seek to minimize push-back through programs of various types to soften up employees' attitudes about the upcoming conversion.

Our approach at Steelcase to managing change has been different (see "Communicating During Change: Be Interactive, Be Participative!" *Target,* First Quarter 2001, pp. 30–33 and the AQP article noted at the end of the box). We provide information about conversion, more frequently in areas that will be most directly affected. Beyond that, we've focused on preparing those in shop floor leadership positions to respond effectively to peoples' questions about the lean conversion, to share briefly the pertinent information about lean, and to solicit further questions from employees. Think of this as a "pull" approach to managing change in which employees' questions and concerns largely establish the agenda and topics.

As the changes in the production system begin to be implemented, we follow the principle that technical change must come before and drive cultural change. So, we focus on clearly communicating the expectations associated with the newly-changed production process. And, we continue to encourage and respond to "pull" signals from employees for more information as the new processes affect their work.

Throughout the lean conversion process, our emphasis on change management has been to prepare shop floor leaders to lead the conversion to lean in their own words (but based on shared understanding of lean principles) largely prompted by employee questions. In units with strong, effective, responsive leadership employee resistance simply has not been an issue. In units with less effective leadership, resistance has been problematic. And, in units where we've changed leaders, employee attitudes toward lean and the change to it have followed suit.

A second crucial influence on employees' attitudes is the degree to which management follows through on the lean principle calling for experiments to be carried out at the lowest possible level in the organization under the guidance of a leader/teacher (see Spear and Bowen's excellent article on the rules of the Toyota Production System). When leaders provide avenues to implement employees' suggestions for process changes and improvements, the effect on attitudes is powerfully positive, far beyond what any "attitude" or "morale" program could hope to produce.

To sum up, attitude is a lot like culture. Both arise from the habits and practices in the management system. In fully-implemented lean management systems, most employees will feel able to be heard when they want to be, and most will believe they have a bona fide opportunity to influence the production processes in which they work. When you establish these two conditions, employee attitude will take care of itself.

Mann, D.W., "Why Supervisors Resist Change and What You Can Do About It," Journal of Quality and Participation, 2000, 23, 3.

Spear, S., and H.K. Bowen, "Decoding the DNA of the Toyota Production System," Harvard Business Review, September-October, 1999, pp. 96–106.

- Jump onto the line or expedite parts when things slow down, or throw in more people; meet the schedule!
- Always reorder more than the actual need when handling shortages just to be sure you get enough.
- Use an informal gauge of queue size; always keep the line full in case something goes "flooey."
- Approach people who are standing idle and ask them to get back to work.

You can think of many more once you start to see work habits and practices as ... well, as habitual. There's nothing wrong with habits and habitual practices as such. We need them to make the workday more efficient. What's important to remember is that *work-related habits are just as difficult to change as personal habits!*

EXTINGUISHING VERSUS BREAKING HABITS

It's helpful to think in terms of the technical language from behavioral science used in connection with changing habits. The term is not "break." Instead, psychologists use the term "extinguish" when talking about changing habits. Extinguish implies a process, something that occurs gradually over time rather than an event producing a suddenly-changed state. Because of that, extinguish also implies a change that can be reversed under certain conditions. Think of Smokey the Bear's rules: Douse a campfire with water, stir the coals and turn them over, then douse it again. If you don't follow these rules, you run the risk that the campfire can rekindle itself from the live embers you failed to extinguish.

And so with habits. They linger, waiting for the right conditions to assert themselves again. We've seen this kind of thing mere days or weeks following implementation of new lean layouts. Here are some actual examples of old habits reasserting themselves in areas newly-converted to lean layouts: Build up some inventory; allow longer or extra breaks; send people off a balanced line to chase parts or do rework; work around the problem today and let tomorrow take care of itself; leave improvement to "the experts" rather than wasting time on employee suggestions; leave the tracking charts untended and out of date; and so on.

To sum it up, you don't need a different management system for lean because lean is so *complex* compared to what you've done before. You need it because lean is so *different* from what you've done before. Many of the habits in your organization as well as your own are likely incompatible with an effectively-functioning lean production environment. You have a conventional mass production management system and culture. You need a lean management system and culture. How do you go about making that change? We've identified four broad elements that taken together lead to a transformation in culture from mass to lean. They are:

1. Establish standards and accountability for following them
2. Closely monitor the production process and its supporting activities
3. Insist on data-based understanding of variations in process performance
4. Take action — remedial and root cause — to minimize variation in performance.

CONCLUSIONS: CULTURE SUSTAINS THE GAINS

Because lean production is a system, it doesn't matter where implementation starts, as James Womack recently observed. Eventually you'll get to all of the elements. But, sequence does matter when implementing the technical elements and the management, or cultural, practices.

We've learned that technical change must precede cultural change. Technical changes create the need for changed management practices. More than that, lean management doesn't stand on its own. Without the physical changes in flow and pull and the takt-based predictability they permit, production will continue to operate in an environment of daily crisis. How to track flow interrupters when there's no takt-balanced standardized work, no flow? How to assess material replenishment performance without standard lot sizes or resupply times?

ASK THESE QUESTIONS

So, start with the physical technical changes, but don't implement them by themselves. Just as cultural changes don't stand well by themselves, neither do technical changes. Every technical change requires cultural changes — the support of new management practices — in order to maintain its integrity over time. If that's not a law of nature, it's darn close to it! Each time an element of the lean production system is implemented, the elements of the management system to sustain it should also be implemented.

As a check, each time a technical or physical element of lean is put in place, ask these questions: What's the process to sustain this? What lean management practices must accompany this element to sustain its effectiveness? These questions apply to the full range of changes that come with implementing lean. Figure 1.3 lists a few examples to illustrate the point:

The three questions from the Toyota Production System that guide any gemba (in Japanese, gemba is where the action is; in manufacturing, gemba is the shop floor) walk are:

1. What is the process here?
2. How can you tell if it's working normally?
3. What are you doing to improve it?

Element of Lean Production System	Element of Lean Management System
Pull system supermarket	Supermarket daily/weekly audit process. Visual controls for "to be ordered," "ordered and due," and "overdue" deliveries
Kanban replenishment system	Actual order-by-order replenishment cycle time compared with standard setup plus run time
Flow line balanced to takt time	Hourly or more frequent production tracking versus goal and reasons for missed takts. Daily value stream performances and task followup accountability meeting
Team leaders	Team leader standard work, supervisor and superintendent standard work
Waterspider lineside supply	Timed standardized route audited for on-time performance each cycle
Lean implementation activity of any kind	Daily and/or weekly "gemba" walks with lean teacher making and following up on assignments for improvement

FIGURE 1.3 Illustrative lean management practices corresponding to elements of a lean production system.

Until we establish the habits of disciplined adherence to process, we would do well to adopt the following additions to these questions:

1. What is the process here? *What is the process to monitor and sustain it?*
2. How can you tell if it's working normally? *How is normal operation monitored and verified?*
3. What are you doing to improve the process? *What process will sustain the improvement?*

To recap, it may be that the failure most lean conversions eventually experience has to do with being unaware of the conversion in management systems and culture required for sustained success in lean. That's not a surprise. Lean production emerged from the engineering orientations of Henry Ford and then Taiichi Ohno at Toyota. In both cases, circumstances were such that disciplined lean management practices could be imposed, at least through the 1920s at Ford. In contemporary lean conversions, the recipe for sustained success has to include planned implementation of a new, disciplined lean management system to support the physical conversion to lean. With new management practices to sustain the technical lean implementation, a new culture will arise to support, nourish, and extend the gains.

> **QUESTIONS**
>
> - Have you experienced problems or failures in trying to become lean?
> - Is your organization focused not just on results, but on processes?
> - Do you have a lean management system?
> - Are you challenged by culture inertia? Are you able to extinguish old habits?

David Mann, Ph.D., is responsible for supporting implementation of the lean management system at Steelcase, Inc. He is a previous contributor to *Target* and was a presenter at the AME annual conference held in Toronto, Canada October 2003.

Notes

1. Veteran production supervisors are extremely versatile, able to do the work of engineering, maintenance, quality, production control, sourcing, and local trucking when necessary to meet the schedule.
2. Is there an instinct for inventory? That is, was there something coded into our genes in the distant past before humans learned to cultivate food crops? It seems possible that those who gathered and stored more food supplies than they and their families needed were more likely to have survived to pass this trait down through time to the present day. In any case, the comfort derived from excess inventory seems to be widespread.

2

Leading the Working Culture Revolution

John Woods and Robert W. Hall

IN BRIEF

Sustaining the gains from lean and quality initiatives has become a challenge for many companies that have started their journey. However, organizations need to advance their gains, not just hold them, and in more areas than operational process improvement. Leading this effort at the top of the organization is a different kind of leadership, a difference that needs to be understood. Possessed of that understanding, leaders can begin creating further transformation of their working cultures.

Compared with today, operations in North America had a more focused challenge in the 1980s: Compete with Japanese on cost, quality, and technology. They began digging out of that hole with teams, quality, and lean. However, those solutions are becoming a requirement for staying in business. The bar is being raised.

Today, globalization presents a bigger jumble of threats. Cost competition from China and other developing areas can lead to financial disaster so fast that it grabs attention. Beyond that comes a host of other challenges, so many that they are difficult to package in a cohesive mental wrapper (see A Short List on the next page).

To that list many readers will add the challenge of sustaining gains from continuous improvement. Creating a superior work culture is a "sleeper" that might not make the list, although doing so strengthens the ability to tackle all other challenges. A strong, capable organization is more likely to make headway on many challenges at once.

When financially sick, near bankruptcy, the conventional business prescription is cost cutting and tight cash control. However, a once-healthy organization near death probably has processes afflicted with chronic wasting diseases — or it never developed enough vigor to cope with serious threats. Long-term wellness calls for a preventive regimen: rigorous quality, lean operations, agility, innovation, and environmental sustainability — and an organizational culture that thrives on them rather than being allergic to them.

Many companies have made initial improvement using "excellence techniques," but have trouble sticking to the new regimen until it becomes habitual. The intent of almost all these techniques is to develop an organization — people — to wring the waste out of any work process quickly and to be innovative on top of that. No one ever reaches perfection because challenges are always changing.

A Short List of 21st Century Operating Challenges

- Global competition; "surprises" from anywhere
- Energy costs and shortages
- Materials costs and shortages
- Contracts including routine price reductions
- More variety at lower cost
- Expectation of fast-response flexibility
- Operational IT systems (starting with RFID)
- Health care costs and complexity
- Retirement plan obligations
- Threatened industries (airlines, etc. — and suppliers)
- Marketing clutter (spam is only a symptom)
- Shorter product life cycles
- More complex customer service and field service
- Quality is a "given"
- Environmental sustainability (not going away).

Everyone can add to this list. The half-life of a business model is becoming shorter, and "comfort zones" smaller.

The first phase of transformation is learning the techniques. For example, the typical kaizen blitz is a technique learning experience as well as a process improvement project. Limiting the objective to achieving the benefits that come merely from learning the techniques is failing to live healthily after trimming the waste from prior process neglect. If we think that "we've done that," it's easy to revert to old habits, giving up on training because we never got in the game.

The second phase, going for B-Class in Figure 2.1, strives to become a can-do organization. Everyone uses process improvement tools habitually, as part of the culture — what we routinely do around here. Once embedded in how everyone thinks, process improvement is less dependent on projects directed to problem areas, although that continues. Remedial process learning matures into innovative learning, extending inward, into every activity from product development to finance, and outward, to customers and suppliers, imaginatively creating trouble for competitors.

The entire organization shifts from an operative control mentality to a problem-seeking mentality. Creating high process visibility makes problems easy to see. However, seeing problems has no benefit if people only look at them, unable, unauthorized, or unwilling to tackle them. Loosening this psychological choke point is impossible in a company functioning in a business-as-usual mind set. The accounting system doesn't fit. Auditors can't comprehend it. IT systems don't support it. Marketing incentives undermine it. Human resource policies aren't fully compatible. Management wants the product shipped — now. A bank or the board is alarmed by "loss of control."

To succeed, transformation of the working culture has to include everyone. Otherwise, part of the organization is developing a culture different from the rest. This leads to conflict and misunderstanding. Often the new culture is blamed, and the old one forces the changes to be pushed out.

To be sustained, the transformation has to extend beyond the initial implementation objectives of improving cost, quality, and leadtimes. An excellent organization stretches after every challenge in the bullet points above, and more. To survive in global competition from a high-cost region, an organization can't rely on beating every low-cost bid for commodities produced offshore. No matter how efficiently made, that strategy doesn't sustain the margins to be innovative, environmentally responsible, and provide extras for both employees and customers. That is, there's more to excellent performance than "leaning" your way to success.

To create a culture like this, leaders must demonstrate the way, becoming a role model for how to work together, how to learn together, and how to improve performance as measured by many yardsticks. There are many kinds of leaders with many differing approaches to leadership. Not all are

Organization Class	Process Improvement	Innovation	External Responsibility
		Between C-Class and B-Class is a Big Working Culture Gap	
A. Change Resilient	Mastery of process improvement eliminates waste from all-new processes very quickly	Capable of transforming its industry; able to adopt new business models	Unifying social mission serves all stakeholders well; aggressively adapts to rapid changes
B. Habitually Learning	Autonomous improvement and process learning embedded in working culture	Innovate by rigorously learning all base technology; everyone involved in NPD	'Outside-in'; focused on customer needs; very attentive to external environment; balances all stakeholders' needs
		Working Culture Gap	
C. Structured Flow Operations	Core operations integrated; improvement is directed; still coaching tools	New product or service development is project-structured; cross-functional collaboration on projects	Good basic service to customers; good cost-quality-delivery; good 'corporate citizen'

Regular *Target* readers will recognize this as the short version of a system to rate the status of working culture development that has appeared in several prior articles. It's not a precise quantification, like a financial report, nor a process assessment, like Baldrige or Shingo. It classifies the capability level which people in the organization have attained. And it assumes that they are engaged in, or aspire to, process improvement and rapid innovation.

C is the first learning stage of a tightly integrated, highly effective operating organization. Most lean implementations stop at C class. B-Class is a culturally integrated operating business unit. A company can "go for" B Class, but only after surviving the gales of major change can one be sure of having arrived at A-Class (somewhat like being sure of what you will do in combat only if you have been there).

The big shift in working culture is between C and B. Perhaps it should be called a migration, because it does not occur quickly. Learning how to work and think differently is not accomplished in a half-day class, but by diligent practice over a lengthy period — usually years.

FIGURE 2.1

wholly suited to the propagation of this kind of working culture. Those who are suited and willing can create a culture that is more likely to generate long-term success for the organization.

LEADERSHIP FOR TRANSFORMING THE CULTURE

At least once in almost any AME meeting, one is apt to overhear a comment like, "I wish my boss was here." Few bosses readily accept lessons from underlings about ideas that clash with their lifelong convictions about how things work, or ought to work.

Most bosses behave as would anyone else in the same situation. If an idea seems radical, we don't take up with it at first hearing, and usually not at first sight either. A prudent boss is not going to bet the company on something like lean manufacturing, Six-Sigma, or set-based product development that she does not understand. But being open-minded as well as prudent, she might have someone in the organization try it on a small scale, so we can see if we like it. Thus begins many an island of improvement. Others begin as unsanctioned demonstration projects, hoping that success will convince upper management of their merit. And if a CEO sees process improvement as a set of techniques only to improve manufacturing, and having many other concerns, she will delegate the championing of that program.

Regarding the fix as merely a matter of adopting techniques is the beginning of problems. A technique leader is expected to develop a project plan, which is then funded for training and consultants, and perhaps a few other things. Once launched, the non-involved learn about it from a distance, probably as a big program, but just one among several, each competing for funds and attention. The basic working culture does not change.

By co-opting the non-involved, a good technique champion gains enough support to make a good deal of difference. The top management agrees that it's a good approach. Quality goes up, leadtimes come down, and teams rack up an impressive string of kaizen projects. Then what? With the project over, enthusiasm wanes and old habits start creeping back in. The working culture never changed very deeply, and absent a few champions, easily slides back into the habits of business-as-usual.

If changing working culture of an organization is to have direction and be company-wide, the leaders at the top of the company can't be uninvolved. They have to show the way. Ultimately, they deal with all the primary stakeholders, including auditors, bankers, and lawyers — everyone whose non-understanding can derail change for many reasons.

But prospective leaders cannot lead something they don't comprehend, toward goals about which they are unconvinced, for reasons they don't understand. They have to understand the big gap between C-Class and B-Class in Figure 2.1 to generate the will to see this through personally, learning to role model the working dedication and behavior that are expected. That role they can't delegate. Training yes, process change yes; but not exemplifying the working culture change. To exemplify the behavior, they must start to regard the company more as the locus of people who make things work, and less as a legal, financial entity, structured to make money (although cash flow is no less important). Financial results start to become one more necessary outcome among many, rather than a dominant goal overriding all others.

To take this on, most leaders prepare themselves to lead where few companies have ever gone. These aspiring leaders may need to strengthen their capabilities in one or more of four areas (also shown in Figure 2.2):

Understanding Process Excellence: Most leaders comprehend, in the abstract, the benefits of better quality and shorter leadtimes without anyone drawing them a picture. Likewise the value of better products developed faster, or of customer needs understood in great detail, is easy to appreciate. But do they know how to develop these abilities?

Leaders may never have experienced using process improvement tools, starting with a Value Stream Map. They may never have used any problem-solving logic like PDCA (Plan Do Check Act), engaged in a kaizen blitz, or personally examined what a customer does with their product, much less how that product is disposed of at the end of its life. Without experiencing what people actually do in a continuous learning environment, leaders can't relate to the change in thinking which they hope to promote, or detect which long-established habits may work in opposition to them. Leaders need to use these abilities to improve their own processes as well as to understand the work of others.

To envision the work culture that is needed, leaders need to experience the unspoken communication of a visible work environment, and the discipline needed to hold a process gain once it is demonstrated to be possible.

FIGURE 2.2

Without this, leaders have difficulty envisioning a work culture that integrates inquisitiveness, collaboration, and enduring process improvement.

Becoming a Developer More than a Director: Leaders of an excellent organization constantly stimulate people to grow — to learn more; not by reading the Great Books, but by being carefully observant of work processes. Or customers. Or suppliers. Or the environment about them. These leaders ask questions, "What did we learn from this?" "What did you discover today?" Or even, "Why does this customer buy from us?"

Sam Walton is well-remembered for going around everywhere asking questions, even from competitors, yellow pad at the ready. Most top managers ask questions to check performance to some measure; some relish putting people "on the spot" while doing so. Sam asked questions to learn, out of true curiosity, and not to demonstrate who he was or how much he knew, so he seldom made anyone squirm. That is, Sam Walton led by example without always knowing where he was going or making much pretense about anything.

Better than Sam Walton asking questions is an organization full of Sams, each curious about what's going on and how to make things better. That's ideal; everyone can't become that way, but a top-notch working culture is a learning culture stimulating questioning of what is done and how it is done, while maintaining an operating process discipline that allows the questions to lead to systematic change. That's more like a Toyota than a Wal-Mart.

A pretentious, insecure leader can't create such a culture. He has to be the real thing, simply be what he is, regardless of prior experience, but set the tone for the organization. Then he has to develop like-minded leaders.

This is not a short-term conversion. It's a pattern of thinking and behavior to get into, and really doing it is different from merely having a concept of what it might be. Of course, some leaders may naturally be inclined to this mode. However, many, if not most, have to lose reliance on displays of status to become a developer of their people. That is, if they have seen themselves as a holder of an office, a financial hawk, or a great expert on the business, or some part of it, they have to get over that.

Learning the behavior to become a genuine leader for an excellent work culture without doubt requires the most personal courage to undertake. Few of us want to admit that we personally might need a little rework.

Strategic Direction: A company having a great internal metamorphosis is also likely to need a strategic one — a change in direction. Leadership often underestimates how carefully this should be worked out. In many stable, old companies, strategic planning is an off-site review prior to developing the annual budget. Any document that comes out may thereafter receive much less attention than the budget, and the strategy many not be clearly communicated to the troops. The company is more likely to be surprised than to surprise competitors.

However, a question-asking, improvement-minded workforce won't be quiescent about fuzziness of direction. They expect openness, and a minor role in shaping strategy, or at least its implementation, which is the idea behind hoshin kanri. Generic vision statements convey little meaning. Rather than aiming to be "the world's best in your industry," try to succinctly phrase a specific strategy like Komatsu's famed classic: "Surround Caterpillar."

By itself, operational excellence is seldom a sufficient competitive advantage. Strategic direction has to answer the question, "Excellence doing what?" Evaluate threats and opportunities as far on the horizon as one can see them. Devise a mega-plan that promises to capture opportunities and evade threats. Take action on this theme by starting immediate initiatives or revising the goals of ongoing ones (most of these will be separate from ongoing process improvement). Assign leadership responsibilities for new initiatives and be sure to make adjustments based on hoshin feedback from the troops. To contribute to the strategy, they have to think about it and "buy in" too. As the strategy unfolds throughout the organization, it is strengthened and clarified. It aligns everyone in all parts of the organization and gives them the ability to make better daily decisions.

All too often strategic planning is slighted, hung up in denial by senior managers optimistic that a bleak outlook will soon brighten. That's giving in to organizational complacency rather than "making a future for the organization happen."

Structure: An organization is often described only by its org chart. Who reports to whom and what the organizational names are. It is the way many see how they fit in the organization. While this is important for some purposes, structure also implies clarity of responsibility for work processes, who's on first, second, and third, how they cover for each other, and who their back-ups are. Just as payback in lower cycle times from cross-training is significant, the payback in deep, rapid process improvement is significant if one has a self-reinforcing cultural web of responsibility for process discipline and visibility. In a B-Class culture much of this is worked out by teams. Structure and process visibility clearly identify the go-to persons; shared responsibility creates the reinforcement web.

The structure should define primary roles and responsibilities, reducing wasted energy on who does what, and closing gaps between planners and doers, needs and results. Good old kaizen and process visibility systems dramatically improve working relationships and communication too.

CULTURAL ASSUMPTIONS RUN DEEP

As can be seen in the first row of Figure 2.3, B-Class working culture is a major shift in thinking. Cultural assumptions run deep, dredging up concepts buried in brains so long ago that daily work behavior is shaped by ideas not consciously recognized. An old work culture is a "hidden legacy" handed down from long-ago incidents, beautiful and ugly; some never witnessed by anyone now working. And the working culture is also the amalgam of every decision made, large or small, and how it is made.

C-Class Work Culture (more directed)	B-Class Work Culture (more autonomous)	Evidence
Selected Comparisons of the C-to-B Working Culture Change		
Company defined as financial entity; ownership is the dominant stakeholder; goals are monetary	Company is defined as the locus of people that make it work. "Excellent performance" is goal. Try to serve all stakeholders.	External orientation. Many outsiders involved in process improvement, NPD, etc.
Most process improvement is staff initiated (like kaizen events)	Everyone is developed to initiate process improvement	Problem-solving tools (like flip charts) in many gathering areas
Competitive advantage is seen as superior technology/ techniques	Competitive advantage is seen as skilled people communicating easily and learning constantly	Career matrices used? People aspire to become "coaches." Human system visibility as well as process visibility
Complacent – can slack off after a big success	Never complacent – always short of perfection	Adversity and all negative news receive instant attention
Leadership is primarily based on position	Leadership is developed based on experience, trust, and ability to help others develop	People want to follow leaders. Leaders stimulate people to think, learn, and improve
Individuals – especially managers – compete for position	Collaborative learning; compete only to promote progress; all contributions respected	Top leaders regularly and frequently interact with everyone they can feasibly meet
Jump to conclusions; big "bias for action"	Scientific method, with careful observation of reality, has become the "gut level approach"	Evidentiary systems are obvious Reality-based facts and data drive decisions
Project-based innovation of new offerings (NPD)	Innovation of new offerings (or NPD) based on accumulated knowledge	Technology is routinely explored in preparation for NPD projects. Knowledge management system
Environmental sustainability is an afterthought	Environmental sustainability factors into all major decisions	Do any actions project beyond compliance, or ISO 14000?

The transition from C-Class to B-Class culture is from a culture of structured doing to one of constantly learning to do better. From strategy development to daily work, this is a shift in basic thinking, and in habits of work. Such a gut level change does not happen quickly because the assumptions underlying nearly every basic "policy" of an organization will change. This table of comparisons could be ten times as big and still be incomplete because there is no end point — no state at which you've clearly arrived, and then you're done. Rather this is a change in a mode of progressing.

FIGURE 2.3

To move to a new culture requires open questioning of all aspects of the business. Old ways need to be questioned and improved as needed. As positions are filled, the hiring criteria must be broadened to not only include the skills for today, but those skills that will help the organization build its culture for the future.

The hope is that a broader mix of talent, technology, and techniques enthusiastically recombined in a different culture will create an organization that wins against its competition and creates a positive and healthy winning environment for the employees. But a more autonomous, habitually learning organization is basically an organization with different rules, one in which everyone uses their minds and talents every chance they get, not just sporadically, and it's more than talk. That describes B-Class working culture.

Such long-term engagement in the challenges of a company assumes a culture with a low turnover workforce, and a work environment that stimulates people to "go for it." It is not an atmosphere of party-type fun, but accomplishment fun. Studies of human motivation indicate that "intrinsic enjoyment of work" is a major factor in "life satisfaction." Life satisfaction isn't short term, and those who find their work absorbing are more productive and creative.[1]

Technical and manufacturing enterprises striving to excel in meeting all the challenges at the beginning of this article need to go for B-Class working culture, not only moving beyond strict functional bureaucracy, but beyond the hidden assumptions that come with it. Every organization, like fast food outlets, doesn't need this, but manufacturers intending to survive in global competition do.

LEADERSHIP FOR CULTURAL CHANGE

Working cultures take on the characteristics of top leadership, if only to assume their mannerisms and the performance measures they dictate. The leadership needs to stimulate a big change in how people think at work, a long-term evolution. Surface changes, even with lean operations, don't dive deep enough. Leaders have to role model the work behavior they expect. If they don't know how, they have to learn. Once started down that path, they must make sure the organization learns also. This is done by a combination of leading by example and training.

This sounds more complicated than it is; just takes practice asking the right kinds of questions. If you're the leader, keeping four points in mind may help:

1. Direct people only when you must; otherwise stir them to learn on their own. Ask lots of questions: "What did you see happening today?" "Have we thought of a way to keep this from happening again?" "What would a customer think?" And after an improvement, "Great! What did we learn that we can use on the next round?"

2. Develop senior or experienced people to also shift toward mentoring, asking questions more than directing. In that way, develop leadership throughout the organization.

3. Create "learning discipline," so that effective learning builds on itself. In production, that's holding standard work (or standardized work); everyone experimenting with everything at once is confusing. In engineering, ask how we can re-use what we've learned and make it better on the next project. Learning is the result of making controlled changes and *everyone* monitoring the effect.

4. Encourage experience outside the company. As much as is feasible, enable the interaction of all employees with customers, suppliers, and even auditors and regulators. An "outside-in" company is more likely to satisfy customers and other stakeholders — and to influence them toward its offerings.

Leadership development includes more, of course. Learning to role model may require more subtle behavioral adjustment than asking questions. Some leaders, by force of old habits, undermine their own initiatives without realizing that they are doing it.

AME LEADERSHIP PROGRAM

In 2005, AME initiated a program to coach leadership toward a B-Class culture, addressing the issues raised in this article. We started by promoting one-day overview programs to create understanding in a little more depth. Senior leaders could then follow up with more extensive programs being developed to address each of three key areas: Understanding process excellence, Leadership to develop other people, and Strategic direction of a strong culture organization. Structure of responsibility was woven throughout.

However, stagnation of organizations at C-Class is a serious problem. No one need wait on a formal program to start leading their company toward a B-Class working culture.

QUESTIONS

- What are the biggest challenges facing your business today?
- How would you rate the status of your working culture development?
- Is your top leadership involved in changing the culture? Do they understand process excellence? Do they set strategic direction?
- Does your structure clearly define roles and responsibilities?

John Woods was vice president of corporate quality and held other manufacturing and engineering positions at Storage Technology, where he also engaged in leadership development programs. He is AME's new director of our leadership initiative.

Robert W. Hall is editor-in-chief of *Target* and a founding member of AME.

REFERENCES

1. See for instance, Robert Lane, *The Market Experience,* Cambridge University Press, 1991, Ch. 20. This is heavy reading, summarizing and integrating many streams of mostly academic research up to that time.

3

Thriving on Continuous Learning at Hewlett-Packard America's Software Manufacturing (ASM): It's more than a strategy — it's their culture

Lea A.P. Tonkin

IN BRIEF

Hewlett-Packard (HP) America's Software Manufacturing (ASM) employees in Nashua, NH not only survived corporate changes but thrived. They're banking on continuous learning and improvement, and can show the results of this successful strategy.

What if you could turn on people's minds, transforming thoughts and unlocking creativity in ways that enhance individual and overall performance? Better yet, can you keep that innovative mind-spring wound up and ticking for years at a time? That might sound a bit fuzzy or flaky to the number-crunchers among us. And yet it is exactly this sort of thinking that created a continuous learning environment at Hewlett-Packard (HP) America's Software Manufacturing (ASM) in Nashua, NH and continues to inspire measurable performance gains. ASM employees provide software for internal HP operations as well as for third party software developers and OEMs. Here's how the HP folks figured out a way to make continuous improvement (CI) *everybody's* business at ASM, and how this approach boosted their customer service and other performance standings.

Selected examples of ASM's 2004CI activities are shown in the box, "ASM Activities/Improvements."

BUILDING A CONTINUOUS LEARNING/IMPROVEMENT CULTURE

ASM employees' willingness to accept the notion of continuous learning and development as part of their job/role likely stems in part from the transitions and uncertainties they've experienced. Bob DiGregorio, plant manager, said, "We started with Digital Equipment, then later a merger by Compaq, and now we are part of HP. We have moved through three very different corporate environments and cultures in a three-year period. Change proved to be the rule, not an exception, for all of us."

ASM ACTIVITIES/IMPROVEMENTS

- Customer FastJIT (ASM's version of kaizen techniques): $19,289 cost avoidance
- Removal of carousel in a high-volume kitting area small group improvement activity (SGIA): $40,907 cost avoidance
- Automated pricing (Green Belt): $100,000 cost savings and $33,000 cost avoidance
- Offsite product master storage (SGIA): $420,000 cost savings
- Transitioned previously-outsourced HP software releases to internal (SGIA): $510,000 cost savings
- ASM shipping carrier automation project (SGIA): $34,763 cost avoidance.

Although employees at the Nashua operation have practiced CI for some time, there's a major difference when it is integrated with continuous learning, according to DiGregorio. "The traditional CI approach was to ensure we kept up with changes and events," he said. "As we continued our focus on continuous learning, we adopted the notion that we need to move ahead of change by providing and creating readiness through learning and development, not just reacting to events. We looked at how a teaching hospital operates, what their work is, and how they learn as they treat patients, and how we can apply these concepts. We adopted the motto, *'The Work Will Teach Us.'*"

Their "ASM University" (or ASMU, an in-house resource — see the later description about ASMU), for example, is not just a program or series of programs, but symbolically represents a way of thinking about learning

and how they can apply these "lessons" in day-to-day activities. "We believe that the way people think affects the way they behave, and in turn impacts our results," said DiGregorio. "We try every day, in every way, to enhance the quality of our thinking. The cumulative effect is that we are thriving on people's minds as they act and react in various situations."

ABOUT HEWLETT-PACKARD'S (HP) AMERICA'S SOFTWARE MANUFACTURING (ASM) IN NASHUA, NH

Software manufacturing and distribution is what 179 full-time employees and more than 250 "Q-Flex" just-in-time workers do at Hewlett-Packard (HP) America's Software Manufacturing (ASM) facility in Nashua, NH. They provide software for internal HP operations as well as for third party software developers and OEMs. ASM supports more than 2600 products. The Nashua facility is approximately 182,000 sq. ft. ASM also encompasses a Fremont, CA plant.

TEAM-BASED, FOCUSED ON OVERALL GAINS

Continuous learning at ASM goes hand-in-hand with their teaming approach — a second critical element in their overall culture. "Everything we do is team-based," said Bob Dufresne, manufacturing/employee engagement manager. "Our philosophy and our activities, through teamwork, help everyone to understand our processes, from front to back. This enables us to merge operating and improving into our daily activities. We do not view ourselves as working in segmented functions within ASM. We share what we do with others because we are all part of ASM, and ultimately HP, in our pursuit of customer satisfaction. Basically, we live in organizations, but work in teams."

Employees are encouraged to participate in OLF (Operations Leadership Forum), which is a "town hall meeting" each Friday. Daily, weekly, and quarterly results are reviewed and discussed, and employees share specific improvements with others. These sessions reflect the operation's value and recognition of CI and learning. CI's grassroots momentum is reflected in smaller, informal improvements that are a natural part of daily activities. "We do as much as we can that's 'quick and effective,'" Dufresne said.

TARGETING SPECIFIC IMPROVEMENTS

Following on continuous learning/CI and team-based activities, a third key element in ASM's successful operation is the alignment to their overarching goals. The corporate hierarchy of integrated goals and objectives was severely impacted as a result of the mergers. "We found ourselves 'disconnected' to the strategic framework of the various companies. As a result, we adopted the Malcolm Baldrige framework, which provided us a disciplined, adaptable, proven, and effective methodology to run our operation," DiGregorio said. "It was a significant milestone in our development."

ASM developed Managing for Results (MFR — see Figure 3.1) as a means to ensure continuing efforts on specific, needed improvements. "We put together a goal-specific integrated roadmap, calling out our key initiatives and strategies each year, based on key ingredients or needs that come from our customers and corporate goals," DiGregorio added.

MFR aligns strategies, goals, and metrics with customer-driven improvement activities. MFR clearly articulates to employees the impact that their individual activities and performance has on overall operating results. MFR provides a methodology and operating network for everyone. MFR teams are aligned with ASM's overarching goals. Each team develops a set of Critical Success Factors, with stretch goals that create gaps used to trigger improvement activities. Individual as well as team knowledge and creativity power these improvement activities. Employees identify gaps, diagnose causes, and are empowered to make required changes for improvements.

ASM's overarching goals are:

- *Loyal customers:* Associates strive to improve and sustain customer service supported by predictability, customer loyalty, customer site visit feedback, delivery, quality, and other factors.
- *Inspired people:* CI participation and performance plans for teams and individuals contribute to employee "inspiration." Also important are recognition, learning effectiveness tracking, employee satisfaction (ASM has consistently exceeded corporate averages in all categories such as communications, teamwork, rewards and recognition, and development), leadership effectiveness (360degree reviews, for example), effective communications, community/employee events, and other areas.

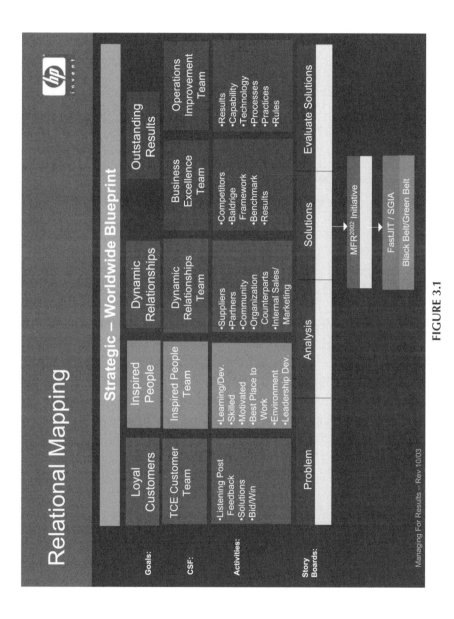

FIGURE 3.1

- *Best cost:* Asset management is carefully and continuously monitored. Among their measurables are inventory turns, freight cost, business system availability, resource utilization (effective use of people on a just-in-time [JIT] basis), capital cycle count, and spending.
- *Outstanding results:* Reflect day-by-day, all-out attention to operating results.

Visibility management is very important. Each area displays the major metrics and results they utilize to monitor their group's performance, and also their tie into ASM's overall metrics.

VOICE OF THE CUSTOMER

Searching for even more effective ways to build their business, ASM listens to the "voice of their customers" through surveys, day-to-day contact, and formal business reviews. ASM has developed an effective process that allows customers the opportunity to provide timely feedback, suggestions, and enhancements.

ASM has set aggressive goals in the area of customer satisfaction/loyalty. Its goals and metrics target levels associated with benchmarked best-in-class companies.

Along with listening to the voice of their customers, ASM also participates in HP's annual "Voice of the Workplace" surveys. "The results of this comprehensive survey provide us with much-needed information regarding what areas we need to address," said DiGregorio. "This formal survey, in conjunction with ASM's ongoing communications and feedback programs, ensures we are all in synch regarding expectations."

ASMU: EVERYONE'S LEARNING

ASMU is the Nashua operation's employee development program. "ASMU is the method we use for the creation and ongoing management of knowledge capital within ASM," said Dufresne. (See Figure 3.2.) Through ASMU, they want to develop and sustain knowledgeable, committed workers who can nimbly keep ASM on a world-class pathway. The program features

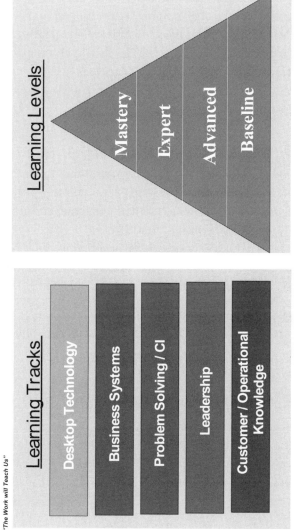

FIGURE 3.2

learning modules designed to help employees meet current and future needs identified through corporate/customer/employee feedback loops. All employees are encouraged to consider courses that will help them build and develop the skills that will keep them not only current with their roles, but equally important, viable for future work, according to Dufresne.

Four learning levels offer employees the opportunity to start at the beginning (baseline) in any particular study area and progress through advanced, expert, and then mastery levels of achievement. The ASMU "learning tracks" dovetail with MFR learnings and experience to match current and projected needs and address any training gaps that have been identified by the Learning Council.

Learning tracks for personal development and training and selected course offerings within them include:

- *Desktop Technology:* PC skills, PowerPoint, Excel, Meeting Tools, Super User Training
- *Problem Solving/CI:* Green Belt, data collection and analysis, Q-Basics (baseline quality training), FastJIT
- *Leadership:* ethics, coaching skills, negotiation skills, business writing
- *Customer, Operational, and Business Systems Knowledge:* HP Customer Connection, lead assessor training, basics of print, finance overview.

A Learning Council oversees ASMU and is composed of all levels in the organization. ASM has 64 internal ASMU "faculty" (employees trained in specific coursework) who develop and deliver the classes.

Employees informally add their suggestions for coursework that can help them progress in customer service and other areas. A formal, annual survey also draws comments on needed training.

"We believe that everyone here is a potential leader," said Dufresne. "We all need customer, operational, and business systems knowledge. We ensure learning in areas to move the business forward, and we measure that progress." Instructor and course performance are also measured.

MORE LEARNING, IMPROVEMENT TOOLS

Trained in problem-solving, leadership, post-sale technologies, and other areas, ASM employees are assisted by Green Belt and Black Belt improvement specialists within their ranks. They are also armed with kaizen (fast-track improvement) techniques, and coached by managers who keep an eye on problem-solving progress, enabling *everyone* in the ASM operation to accept accountability for making day-by-day improvements. Ninety-two percent of their employees participated in CI activities during the past year.

Among the customer satisfaction and productivity-boosting tools employed at ASM are *demand-driven execution* (continuous flow toward customers, finding ways to slice response times); *root cause analysis* (eliminating problems through cross-functional activities); and *MFR* (as described earlier, it is customer-focused CI and problem-solving activities); and *continuous learning* through ASMU and other programs.

An added "tool" employed here is JIT staffing — called "Q-Flex." The program aims to put trained people where and when they are needed, operating on a JIT basis. Approximately 225 employees work as needed on a part-time basis. They are valued as reliable and cost-effective contributors to first-rate customer service.

LEADERSHIP EDGE

Leadership effectiveness among all employees gives ASM a competitive edge. "We use 360-degree feedback for measuring leadership performance," said Dufresne. "We all need to walk the talk, not asking people to make changes that we would not make ourselves. We ask people to be CEOs of their work areas." For example, ASM senior managers participate in the 360-degree feedback process. As a result, individual leadership development needs are identified and action plans created in conjunction with their manager. These improvement plans are then incorporated into the individual manager's formal performance/development plan and are reviewed on a regular basis to monitor progress.

DiGregorio noted that all of these efforts carry ASM along a competitive path — yet there are no guarantees of lifelong success in their markets. "What motivates us to learn and do the things we do? We have survived in three company cultures," he said. "The era of life-long employment is gone. The world we live in now is very different. What we offer is *employability* — to be able to adapt and work in different situations. We are not laser-beaming on simply keeping today's jobs. We are paying attention to the leadership development and learning that our employees and our business will require in the future."

QUESTIONS

- Do you integrate continuous learning with continuous improvement?
- Do you have a team-based approached to continuous improvement?
- Does your organization have clear, overarching goals?
- Do you strive to hear the voice of the customer?

Lea A.P. Tonkin, *Target* editor, lives in Woodstock, IL.

4

Batesville Casket Company's Culture of Continuous Improvement: Innovation, creativity — and yes, listening to the voice of the customer — are alive and well here

Lea A.P. Tonkin

IN BRIEF

Batesville Casket Company's been listening to the "voice of the customer" for many years. The article describes their Daily Continuous Improvement culture, employee involvement, metrics, and lessons learned as they contribute to progress.

There must be zillions of ways to build a casket. Fancy with all the trimmings, inscribed with the departed's favorite poem, lined with silky fabrics, decorated with original artwork, constructed of special materials (wood selections from walnut to poplar, pecan, etc. or metals such as bronze, stainless steel, and copper) — or perhaps more basic and unadorned. Whatever the request (although their final customers may not have much to say about it), Batesville Casket Company associates know just how to do it right and ship it on time, with as much creativity as the customer calls for.

Although customer satisfaction surveys reflect consistently high ratings, Batesville associates do not accept today's domestic marketplace leadership performance as their "final resting place." Thanks to their employee involvement and continuing performance improvements, they plan on even better customer satisfaction and market success. This article offers insights Batesville employees shared during a recent AME workshop, "Creating a Culture of Continuous Improvement," at the company's operation in Batesville, IN.

CREATIVITY AND CUSTOMIZATION

"Innovation and creativity are alive and well at Batesville Casket Company," said Gary Lambert, director of manufacturing. "Finish and function are important to our customers," Lambert said. "We offer a customization service for special requests. For example, inside the lid, or the 'cap panel' as we call it, you can have these special panels embroidered with designs such as a picture, poem — anything you can imagine that can be imprinted with various colors and textures."

Themed corner hardware, optional drawers built into caskets to hold papers and other personal items, and many other custom options are available. In addition to 500+ casket styles, Batesville offers a wide variety of cremation urns and containers, with new product ideas continually in the works.

DAILY CONTINUOUS IMPROVEMENT CULTURE

Batesville associates work together in what they describe as a "Daily Continuous Improvement culture," or DCI (see Figure 4.1). It's an effective way to connect shop floor operations — all operations — with corporate strategy. Asked how it works, Lambert said, "We believe that CI is based on *need* and without need, there can be no CI. Production expectations that are challenging (stretch targets), clear and visibly tracked, create this need."

Lambert continued, "The majority of our improvements come from DCI activities. Individuals or small groups who are trained in lean concepts and who work on very targeted issues such as specific safety, quality, cost, and service challenges, accomplish these."

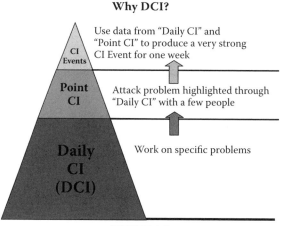

FIGURE 4.1

ABOUT BATESVILLE BASKET COMPANY

Batesville Casket Company, a Hillenbrand Industries subsidiary, is a top manufacturer of metal and hardwood caskets in the United States. The Batesville, IN-based operation also offers cremation urns and caskets. Employees pride themselves on the beauty and quality of their workmanship. Batesville Casket has five plants in five states and employs more than 3500 people including 900 at the Batesville, IN facility.

The company history goes back quite a ways. Batesville Coffin Company had been in business since 1884, a small-town operation where employee hand-made wooden coffins known for ornate engravings. In 1906, John A. Hillenbrand crafted high-quality hardwood coffins and caskets (caskets are rectangular boxes and coffins are six-sided with a top and bottom narrower than the middle). Demand increased as he invested in modern woodworking machinery and added a power plant for a larger operation. Reliable delivery and a brood line of products helped to build customer loyalty over the years.

Hillenbrand's son, John W. Hillenbrand, later assumed leadership for business marketing and financial development. Another son, George C. Hillenbrand, further advanced automation in the factory and brought in engineering as well as R&D expertise from outside the company. In 1918, Batesville Casket retooled and began fabricating metal caskets, in turn decreasing wooden casket production. Changes in shell shape, interior options, and finishing were dramatic. Their emphasis on superior product and service quality continued.

Metal casket production ceased when World War II began. The company thrived during the war, turning out wood caskets for military and other customers. They resumed metal casket production in 1948 and dropped wood caskets from their product lineup by 1953. Wood casket manufacturing again started up in 1973.

Among the significant milestones cited by the company are: development of the first vacuum testing system in 1948 (all of their caskets must pass multiple vacuum tests); the 1954 introduction of the Memorial Record™ tube (an identification method without distributing the casket interior); Cathodic Protection launched in 1958 (helps to prevent corrosion on the steel casket surface); warranty introduction in 1963, an industry first; the Living Memoria® program, which has grown to be the largest private U.S. reforestation program; and the company's Failsafe® liner which protects hardwood caskets from damage caused by interior fluids.

Personalization within funeral services gained popularity in the 1990s, and Batesville Casket continued to evolve, paced by customer demand. Among their personalized offerings are interior panel designs (cap panels) reflecting different cultures, hobbies, faiths, etc.; MemorySafe® drawers built into selected wood and metal caskets, allowing families a personal memorial that can be open privately; and the Life Symbols® interchangeable corner hardware for various metal and wood caskets. Cremation products and services are in the newest product line. More information about the company and its products, services, and history is available at its website (www.batesville.com).

Batesville employees use "Point Kaizens" when added resources are needed to resolve issues. "These involve small groups meeting for two to three days," Lambert said. "When issues are still more complex or broader in scope, full kaizen week-long events are utilized." He noted that steps in creating the culture include trainings in: lean manufacturing principles; problem-solving techniques; and group interaction skills.

VOICE OF THE CUSTOMER

Internal customers include more than 80 distribution sites (service centers). External customers are licensed funeral homes; final customers are buyers of their caskets and other products/services.

A focus on the customer and long-term commitment to improvement are well known for Batesville Casket. After years of working on improvement activities, how do they keep this approach "fresh?" Lambert said, "As a manufacturing organization, we use numerous data streams to understand the voice of the customer, including routine surveys, written and phone comments. We also provide a feed-back card (customer satisfaction survey) in the casket, and get a good response rate. The great majority of comments we receive are very favorable. We also provide regular customer visits by plant personnel, and customers offer feedback during regular visits to our plants."

POLICY DEPLOYMENT

Translating customer requirements into better overall performance requires effective policy deployment and metrics —connecting the dots to the shop floor and other areas. Lambert explained, "The process starts at a corporate level with our vision, mission, and strategic initiatives. Cascading from those are supporting initiatives at each level of the organization that are linked to the strategic initiatives. Individual performance measurement and compensation are then linked to these more specific initiatives.

METRICS

All associates understand how their day-by-day performance supports the company's overall performance. Their key metrics are focused on safety, quality, cost, and delivery. "As we define our goals and targets under each of these, we will address any gaps that appear," Lambert said. "For example, a cost problem may develop at the plant level, and in turn a DCI activity is created. If that doesn't solve the problem, we may have a two to three-day event with people from various plants and functions evaluating the problem, as needed." He added that specific individual and organizational development initiatives are enablers that support initiatives within the safety, quality, cost, and delivery categories.

"At the plant level, detailed measurements occur daily," Lambert said. "Weekly, we have combined one-hour net-meetings to review approximately ten standard measurements for each of the six plants. This provides a forum for sharing of information as well as identifying issues and corrective action in a timely manner."

All administrative as well as production personnel learn about Batesville Casket goals, metrics, and culture in an initial orientation at each location. It includes an eight-hour training class in the principles of lean manufacturing. A progressive simulation game is used to facilitate the learning.

LESSONS LEARNED

Most every company has "lessons learned" they are willing to share with others as they continue along the improvement path. Lambert noted, "The list below is a partial list of critical success factors. Some we already knew and some we learned the hard way."

- Educate "top-down" and then forever practice what has been learned.
- Focus on the quality of events versus quantity.
- Demonstrate conviction and "stay the course."
- Learn from mistakes and celebrate successes.
- Measure the things that are important.
- Consistently practice standard work. There can be no kaizen without it!
- Good training processes are critical. If the associate hasn't learned, the instructor hasn't taught!

- Stay focused on the "significant few" areas that matter most to your customers.

LOOKING AHEAD

What's next for Batesville Casket? "One of our biggest initiatives over the next couple of years is to 'sharpen the saw,' again from the top down, to reinforce our fundamental skills," Lambert said. "We will be piloting a six-week, full-time development class that focuses on lean principles. This class has been condensed from a 12-week program. Good progress has been made to implement lean principles in non-manufacturing areas as well; however, this is still an area of opportunity."

QUESTIONS

- Do you use different types of kaizen events to achieve improvements?
- Do you have a process for policy deployment?
- What key metrics do you use? Do all employees understand how their performance affects the company's overall performance?
- Do you learn from mistakes and celebrate successes?

Lea A.P. Tonkin, Woodstock, IL is the editor of *Target* magazine.

5

5S at Deceuninck North America's Monroe Site: Sustaining and Improving the Gains: 5S is the foundation for culture change and continuing improvements

Cash Powell Jr. and Steve Hoekzema

IN BRIEF

This article describes how associates at Deceuninck North America (DNA) in Monroe, OH, learned that 5S is not just about orderliness, cleanliness, and standardizing work areas. 5S is about changing a culture, establishing the discipline, changing work habits, and developing a new way of thinking. Productivity, safety performance, and other gains resulting from this approach have been significant, as well as the realization that continuing focus on 5S on a daily basis is needed to sustain and build upon these improvements.

The management team at the Monroe, OH facility of Deceuninck North America (DNA), formerly Dayton Technologies,[1] has learned that 5S is not just about orderliness, cleanliness, and standardizing work areas. 5S is about changing culture and work habits while establishing the disciplines to develop a new way of thinking.

When Mike Hutfless, DNA's COO, first introduced 5S in 1999, many people expressed concern for the money spent on the process. As a former U.S. Navy officer, Hutfless knew the operational positives of maintaining an organized work environment — an area where associates could immediately locate tools and wouldn't trip over clutter. DNA believes sustaining such a well-organized work environment is the fundamental requirement for ongoing continuous improvements (CI) in other areas of manufacturing.

5S is an essential path on DNA's journey to becoming a world-class organization. The disciplines used to organize and properly maintain a work area encompass the same traits needed to make an organization world-class. To emphasize this point, Director of Operations Steve Hoekzema explained, "If both the associates and managers of a company can't remember or don't make it a priority to return a broom or garbage can to its proper location, how can they effectively operate millions of dollars' worth of production equipment and continuously improve the operation?"

ORGANIZING FOR CHANGE

When the Monroe plant began to implement 5S, management understood that once the first four elements of 5S (Sort, Set in order, Shine, and Standardize) were in place, the area would likely return to its historical clutter if a system were not in place to sustain the gains. This is the reason why the fifth "S" (Sustain) is so crucial to the overall success of the program. Think about how many new programs work great for the first month and then fade off after time. Sustaining is the most difficult of the 5Ss. To sustain, in 5S, means keeping the work area at the required levels.

During the first two years of 5S implementation, the Monroe site appointed a full-time 5S facilitator to develop the training standards, train the 250 associates, and facilitate the 5S teams. A cross-functional implementation team developed an audit checklist.

Once a work area becomes ready to be certified, the auditor conducts the certification inspection which consists of 22 items of inspection categorized by each of the 5Ss (see Figure 5.1). Each work area establishes its own schedule for 5S implementation and readiness for certification. It is prudent to note that a 5S team can move the scheduled due date for certification as long as the team is progressing and the new target date is reasonable.

When the associates in a work area are ready to be certified, the 5S facilitator inspects the area against the standard items illustrated in Figure 5.1. The audit team conducts a two-hour inspection of the work area. Later that day,

Document Title:			Document No.	FRM A-2			
	5S AUDIT RECORD		Revision No. D	Page: 1		Of 2	
Required By: PRO A-1	**Work Area:**			**Audit Date:**			

Audit Type: ☐ Initial Certification   ☐ Sustaining   ☐ Re-Certification

Auditors:

Name: _____   Name: _____

Workplace Representatives:

Name: _____   Name: _____

5S	**Item** (Attach detailed audit results)	Rating Method	**Rating**
	Distinguish between what is needed and not needed:		
1. Sort (Organization)	**A.** 5S Board is posted in the workarea. • Workarea Map, Workarea Audit Scores (KOI Chart), Before & After Pictures and Temporary Storage Contents List. • Pre-audit checklist (FRM A-2 and FRM A-3) and workplace design record posted in workarea (for initial certification audits only).	B	
	B. Unneeded equipment, tools, furniture, etc. are present.	A	
	C. Unneeded items in work area are present.	A	
	D. Unneeded inventory, supplies, parts, or materials are present.	A	
	A place for everything and everything in its place:		
2. Set in Order (Orderliness)	**A.** Correct places for items are not obvious.	A	
	B. Items are not in their correct places.	A	
	C. All modification project items are logged with Facility Engineering.	A	
	D. Height and quantity requirements are not met. • Height & quantity limits are not obvious. • Items do not exceed quantity limits.	A	
	E. Not all piping is labeled with contents and direction of flow.	A	
	F. Items are setting on the floor that does not need to set on the floor.	A	
	G. Safety violations exist. Attach FRM A-3 (5S Safety Audit Record).	C	
	H. Aisles are not established or meet minimum width requirements.	A	
	Clean:		
3. Shine (Cleanliness)	**A.** Floors, walls, stairs, and surfaces are not free of dirt, oil, and grease.	C	
	B. Equipment is not kept clean and free of dirt, oil, and grease.	C	
	C. All cleaning supplies can be located within 30 seconds.	A	
	D. Lines, signs, labels etc. are not clean and unbroken.	A	
	E. Storage location lines do not meet policy requirements.	A	
	F. Facility and equipment color requirements are not met.	A	
	Maintain and monitor the first three categories:		
4. Standardize (Adherence)	**A.** Records showing responsibilities for sort, set in order, and shine are defined and posted in the workarea.	B	
	B. Not everyone in the work area knows when, where, and how to perform 5S responsibilities.	A	
	Stick to the rules:		
5. Sustain (Self-discipline)	**A.** Records do not exist to show that 5S inspections are performed regularly (daily, weekly, monthly, etc.).	B	
	B. All previous 5S audit deficiencies were not corrected.	B	
		Overall	

This document was current on the date of printing (4/9/2008) but may have been revised or discontinued on a subsequent date. Consult the BCS Library to determine if this revision is current.

FIGURE 5.1 Part 1.

Document Title:		Document No:	FRM A-2		
5S AUDIT RECORD		Revision No:	D	Page:	2

Rating

Rating Method A		Rating Method B		Rating Method C	
Number of Discrepancies	Rating	Result	Rating	Number of Discrepancies	Rating
None	4.0	Pass	4.0	None	4.0
1	3.0	Fail	0	1	2.0
2	2.0			2 or more	0
3 or 4	1.0				
5 or more	0				

RECORD OF REVISIONS

Rev. No.	Date of Issue	Revisions
New	10-09-00	NA
A	10-16-00	Added category numbers and letters for item identification.
B	03/15/02	Added pre-audit checklist to 1A and deleted 4C. Added work area to header.
C	11/22/02	Changed items 2F, 3A, and 3B to a rating method of C. Added rating method C to form to put more emphasis on safety and housekeeping.
D	01/16/04	Revised Item 1A to clarify what is required on a 5S board, added 2C: all modification project items need logged with Facility Engineering, Clarified height and quantity requirements in 2D, Added 3D: Storage location lines do not meet policy requirements, Added 3E: Facility and equipment color requirements are not met and revised 5B to read All previous 5S audit deficiencies were not corrected.

DISTRIBUTION:	Original – Audit file. Copy 1 – Area supervisor.

FIGURE 5.1   Part 2.

the audit report, which includes the audit score, a list of non-conformances, and digital pictures of each non-conformance, is published.

All certification inspections result in at least a few non-conformances. In order to become certified, all that is necessary is to correct the issues listed in the audit. Then a follow-up audit is performed and if all of the issues are corrected, the work area receives a perfect score and they become 5S certified. A certified work area reflects the hard work of each individual in the area. Certification is an honor for employees involved in this process. In Monroe, a plaque is awarded to the team of the newly-certified area by DNA management during a celebration ceremony, along with gift certificates for the team members. Since the 5S process was started, 23 out of 27 work areas have been certified.

SUSTAINING THE DISCIPLINE

Once an area has been certified, it is only the beginning of a journey toward other operational improvements. The process of becoming 5S certified is difficult and requires a lot of effort, but the challenge of sustaining the certification is even greater. Once a work group becomes certified, it is common to hear, "Congratulations! Now comes the hard part."

The foundation of the fifth S (Sustain) is unannounced audits. There is an average of three or four sustaining audits per work area each year. The auditor inspects the work area for the same 22 points on the certification audit in Figure 5.1. A passing score on a sustaining audit is at least 3.2 out of 4.0 possible points. A sustaining audit report is then sent to the departmental management group and includes pictures of each of the violations. If the work group disagrees with an audit non-conformance, an appeal may be presented to the auditor. If appropriate, the audit score may be modified; however, the 5S auditor makes the final decision on appeals.

Even if a work area passes the audit with a score of 3.2 or above, violations are fixed and action is taken to prevent recurrence of any stated violation. If the work area fails three consecutive audits, the area is decertified and must then start over with the certification process. Although decertification does not occur often at the Monroe facility, when it does occur, it is taken very seriously. The team in that work area works quickly to identify the cause of the non-conformances and the corrective actions needed.

5S is a high-profile objective for everyone within DNA's Monroe facility. Management receives and comments on all area audits. These comments praise the positive and clarify the importance of the needed improvements. From a performance standpoint, failure to maintain a 5S certification is an indication that the area is not being led properly and priorities are not clear. Performance reviews include both positive and negative comments about the work area's 5S performance.

After a few years of 5S implementation, the position of full-time 5S facilitator transitioned into a part-time audit function. This function takes about eight hours a week to audit the already-certified areas and inspect any areas ready to be certified for the first time. To insure the audit system is sustained, there are three trained auditors qualified to conduct the audits and issue the reports.

BEYOND 5S

In the beginning, employees believed 5S was simply a housekeeping program. As the process expanded into several departments, the efforts which started with cleaning and organizing a workplace developed into changes in work habits, work discipline, and an overall shift in the culture of the organization. When done properly, the message that 5S promotes is, "If you are going to do something, then think it through with the entire work group, plan it well, and do it right." This cultural shift has laid the groundwork for an endless number of improvements in all areas of the business. Listed below are some examples of the general improvements that have occurred since the implementation of 5S.

Empowerment. As the Monroe site developed the 5S audit procedure, the supervisors in each certified area soon learned that in order to sustain the gains, work assignments had to be documented and communicated. For 5S to be effective, each employee must assume ownership of the program in his or her assigned work area. Employees are responsible for specific line items in the 5S audit standard. In a well-implemented 5S program, everyone understands that 5S is an important part of their job and sustaining actions must be done on a daily basis.

Recently, the site discovered a significant cost savings as the result of 5S. While a few extrusion employees were designing a new work area, they realized that a section of material which was sliced off an extrusion profile could no longer be allowed to just fall on the floor. If allowed to fall on the floor, there was a possibility the pieces might block an aisle, which is a safety rule violation. So they designed a method to collect and reuse this material, which resulted in a daily material savings of more than $600. One of the 5S team members said, "We tried to do this 20 years ago, but it was never a high enough priority to fix." As this example illustrates, making 5S a priority in your plant will empower people to make operational improvements.

Environment, Health, and Safety. DNA's Monroe site has not incurred a lost time accident since 5S was introduced. Needless to say, worker's compensation costs have been drastically reduced. DNA believes maintaining discipline and order in the workplace is a strong contributor to their remarkable safety record. As the plant gained experience with the 5S system, such standards as aisle width, standard paint colors for like equipment, ladders and guarding, safety valves, stop buttons, and the like were developed and implemented. John Lakes, a tool maintenance lead, said, "We recently had a small fire in the dumpster. With the work area well marked, it was very clear where the nearest fire extinguisher was located; just look for the red block." Figure 5.2 is an example of Form A-3 with the safety requirements that must be passed as part of the 5S audit. An area that does not adhere to the safety standards will usually fail the 5S audit.

Quality. DNA's Monroe site has a sophisticated, computerized system for controlling their mixing operation. Cleanliness is essential to the high quality of the PVC-U material. The improvement in compound quality in the Monroe plant has helped save $3 million in scrap and rework since the implementation of 5S. In addition, since 1999, the accuracy of shipments has improved from 89.0 percent to 98.5 percent. These are just some of the operational benefits that occur when work areas are better organized, and processes are well documented, standardized, and sustained.

Productivity. Before 5S, searching for tools, supplies, and parts was a significant waste of time. Each associate used a personal toolbox, which in some cases was cluttered, unorganized, and contained a collection of different tools. Because many associates had their own favorite tools for equipment adjustments and setup, variation in machine setups and production output occurred. To obtain a standard work and consistent product quality, the tools and their locations had to be standardized across the work area. This was a difficult change for some associates to accept initially because there were a lot of individual preferences for using their own tools. However, the associates in each work area were involved in deciding what tools should be a standard issue and where they should be located. Including employees in the decision-making process allowed the program to gain acceptance and work more effectively.

Today, the guideline for accessibility of necessary tools, parts, or supplies in each work area is the item should be within a 30-second walk of the work area. At each machine, the toolbox contains only the tools for that machine and all extraneous tools are removed. For common tools such as brooms and shovels, a shadow peg board was placed in each work area, creating a standard location for that item.

It is common in industry to realize a productivity savings of ten percent by eliminating the search for tools. This plant has shown an overall employee productivity improvement of 23 percent since 1999. Hoekzema said that the specific savings associated with 5S improvements are not calculated because the benefits are so obvious they will eventually end up on the bottom line.

Dayton

Document Title:		Document No.	FRM A-3				
5S AUDIT RECORD (SAFETY)		Revision No.	C	Page:	1	Of:	4
Required By: PRO A-1							

Audit Type: ☐ Initial Certification
☐ Sustaining

Auditors: Date: _____
Name: _____   Name: _____
Name: _____   _____
Workplace Representatives: _____
Name: _____   Name: _____

Subject	Questions	Yes	No
1. Aisles	**A.** Are aisles marked? 29 CFR 1910.22(b)(2)		
	B. Are aisle widths maintained? 29 CFR 1910.22(b)(1)		
	C. Are aisles in good condition? 29 CFR 1910.22(b)(1)		
	D. Are aisles and passageways properly illuminated?		
	E. Are aisles kept clean and free of obstructions? 29 CFR 1910.22(b)(1)		
	F. Are fire aisles, access to stairways, and fire equipment kept clear? 29 CFR 1910.178(m)(14)		
	G. Is there safe clearance for equipment through aisles and doorways? 29 CFR 1910.176(a)		
2. Chemicals	**A.** Are all hazardous chemicals appropriately labeled? 29 CFR 1910.1200(f)(5); 29 CFR 1910.1200(f)(6)		
	B. Are workers nearby aware of the content of chemical piping systems? 29 CFR 1910.1200(e)(1)(ii); 29 CFR 1910.1200(f)(5); 29 CFR 1910.1200(f)(6)		
	C. Is there a list of hazardous substances used in your workarea? 29 CFR 1910.1200(e)(1)(I)		
	D. Is there a material safety data sheet readily available for each hazardous substance used? 29 CFR 1910.1200(g)(9); 29 CFR 1910.1200(g)(10)		
3. Electrical	**A.** Do extension cords being used have a grounding conductor? 29 CFR 1910.304(f)(5)(v); 29 CFR 1910.334(a)(3)		
	B. Is sufficient access and working space provided and maintained about all electrical equipment to permit ready and safe operations and maintenance? 29 CFR 1910.303(g)(1); 29 CFR 1910.303(h)(3)		
	C. Are all cord and cable connections intact and secure? 29 CFR 1910.305 (g) (2) (iii)		
	D. Are all disconnecting means legibly marked to indicate their purpose, unless located so that their purpose is evident. 29 CFR 1910.303(f)		
	E. Are flexible (extension) cords and cables free of splices or taps? 29 CFR 1910.305(g)(2)(ii)		

FIGURE 5.2 Part 1.

Document Title:		Document No:	FRM A-3	
5S AUDIT RECORD (SAFETY)		Revision No: C	Page:	2

Subject	Questions		Yes	No
4. Exits	**A.**	Are exits properly marked? 29 CFR 1910.37(q) ; 29 CFR 1910.37 (H)		
	B.	Are exits kept free of obstructions? 29CFR 1910.36(d)(1)		
	C.	Are the directions to exits, when not immediately apparent, marked with visible signs? 29 CFR 1910.37(q)(5)(6)		
	D.	Are doors, passageways or stairways that are neither exits nor access to exits and which could be mistaken for exits, appropriately marked "NOT AN EXIT" "TO BASEMENT," "STOREROOM," etc.? 29 CFR 1910.37(q)(2)		
5. First Aid	**A.**	Do you have emergency eye wash and shower facilities within the immediate work area where employees are exposed to injurious corrosive materials? 29 CFR 1910.151(c)		
	B.	Do you have first-aid kits easily accessible to each work area, with necessary supplies available, periodically inspected and replenished as needed? 29 CFR 1910.151(b)		
	C.	Are emergency phone numbers posted where they can be readily found in case of an emergency? 29 CFR 1910.38 (a)(2)(v)(vi)		
6. Flammable/ Combustible Containers	**A.**	Are approved containers and portable tanks used for the storage and handling of flammable and combustible liquids? 29 CFR 1910.106(d)(2); 29 CFR 1910.144(a)(1)(ii)		
	B.	Are safety cans used for dispensing flammable or combustible liquids at a point of use? 29 CFR 1910.106(d)(5)(iii)		
	C.	Are storage cabinets used to hold flammable liquids, labeled "Flammable—Keep Fire Away"? 29 CFR 1910.106(d)(3)(ii)		
7. Forklift Operations	**A.**	Are all industrial trucks not in safe operating condition removed from service? 29 CFR 1910.178(q)(1)		
	B.	Are your forklifts inspected before being placed in service? Inspections should be at least daily, or after each shift, if used around the clock. 29 CFR 1910.178(q)(7)		
	C.	Are industrial trucks equipped with flashing lights, horn, overhead guard, and name plate (load limits)? 29 CFR 1910.178(a)(2)		
8. Hazardous Waste Management	**A.**	If your operations generate waste from oil or grease, do you handle it in an approved manner? 40 CFR 279.22		
	B.	If your operations generate waste from fluorescent light bulbs, do you handle it in an approved manner? 40 CFR 273.14 (e)		
	C.	If your operations generate hazardous waste, do you handle it in an approved manner according to 40 CFR 262		
9. Hearing Conservation	**A.**	Are workers protected from sources of excessive noise? 29 CFR 1910.95(a)		
	B.	Is approved hearing protective equipment available to every employee working in noisy (where noise levels exceed 85 dBA) areas? 29 CFR 1910.95(i)(1); 29 CFR 1910.141 (a)(3)		
10. Housekeeping	**A.**	Are work areas clean? 29 CFR 1910.22(a)		
	B.	Are mats, grating, etc. used where drainage is needed? 29 CFR 1910.22(a)(2)		
	C.	Is the compressed air for cleaning less than 30 psi? 29 CFR 1910.242(b)		

This document was current on the date of printing (4/20/2005) but may have been revised or discontinued on a subsequent date. Consult the BCS Library to determine if this revision is current.

FIGURE 5.2 Part 2.

Document Title:		Document No:	FRM A-3	
5S AUDIT RECORD (SAFETY)		Revision No: C	Page:	3

Subject	Questions	Yes	No
	D. Are work surfaces kept dry or are appropriate means taken to assure the surfaces are slip-resistant? 29 CFR 1910.22(a)(2)		
	E. Are all spilled materials or liquids cleaned up immediately? 29 CFR 1910.141(a)(3)(ii)		
11. Lockout	**A.** Is all machinery or equipment capable of movement, required to be de-energized or disengaged and locked out during cleaning, servicing, adjusting or setting up operations, whenever required? 29 CFR 1910.147(c)(1); 29 CFR 1910.147(c)(2)(I)		
	B. Are correct lockout/tagout procedures in use? 29 CFR 1910.147(c)(4); 29 CFR 1910.147(d); 29 CFR 1910.147(e)		
	C. Are suspended loads or potential energy (such as compressed springs, hydraulics or jacks) controlled to prevent hazards? 29 CFR 1910.147(d)(5)		
12. Machine Guarding: General	**A.** Are rotating or moving parts of equipment guarded to prevent physical contact? 29 CFR 1910.212(a)(1); 29 CFR 1910.219 (F)		
	B. Are all moving chains and gears properly guarded? 29 CFR 1910.219(f)(1); 29 CFR 1910.219(f)(2)		
	C. Are machinery guards secure and so arranged that they do not offer a hazard in their use? 29 CFR 1910.212(a)(2)		
13. Machine Guarding: Portable Power Tools	**A.** Are grinders, saws, and similar equipment provided with appropriate safety guards? 29 CFR 1910.243(a)(1); 29 CFR 1910.243(c)(1)-(4); 29 CFR 1910.243(e)(1)(I)		
	B. Are power tools used with the correct shield, guard, or attachment recommended by the manufacturer?		
14. Machine Guarding: Stationary Equipment	**A.** Is fixed machinery provided with appropriate safety guard to prevent injuries to the operator and other employees resulting from point of operation, in-going nip point, rotating parts, flying chip, and spark hazards? 29 CFR 1910.212 (a)(1)		
	B. Are foot-operated switches guarded or arranged to prevent accidental actuation by personnel or falling objects? 29 CFR 1910.217 (4)		
	C. Is there a power shut-off switch within reach of the operator's position at each machine? 29 CFR 1910.213(b)(1)		
	D. Are fan blades protected with a guard having openings no larger than ½ in., when operating within 7 ft of the floor? 29 CFR 1910.212(a)(5)		
15. Personal Protective Equipment	**A.** Are all employees required to use personal protective equipment (PPE) as needed? 29 CFR 1910.132(a)		
	B. Is PPE functional and in good repair? 29 CFR 1910.132(e)		
	C. Are all employees required to use personal protective clothing and equipment when handling chemicals (gloves, eye protection, respirators, etc.)? 29 CFR 1910.132(a)		
16. Extinguishers	**A.** Are appropriate fire extinguishers mounted, located, and identified so that they are readily accessible to employees? 29 CFR 1910.157(c)(1)		
	B. Are all fire extinguishers inspected monthly and serviced annually, and noted on the inspection tag? 29 CFR 1910.157(e)		

This document was current on the date of printing (4/20/2005) but may have been revised or discontinued on a subsequent date. Consult the BCS Library to determine if this revision is current.

FIGURE 5.2 Part 3.

Document Title:		Document No:	FRM A-3		
5S AUDIT RECORD (SAFETY)		Revision No:	C	Page:	4

Subject	Questions		Yes	No
17. Walkways	**A.**	Are pits and floor openings covered or otherwise guarded? 29 CFR 1910.22(c); 29 CFR 1910.23(a)		
18. Compressed Gases	**A.**	Are compressed gases properly stored and used? 29 CFR 1910.253(b)(1)–(5)		
	B.	Are compressed gas cylinder storage rules (Dayton Technologies Facility Engineering Drawing 100023) posted in the storage area?		
19. Work Environment	**A.**	Are all work areas adequately illuminated?		
	B.	Are combustible scrap, debris, and waste stored safely and removed from the work site promptly? 29 CFR 1910.141(a)(4)(ii)		

DISTRIBUTION: Original – Audit file. Copy 1 – Area supervisor.

1. **RECORD OF REVISIONS**

Rev. No.	Date of Issue	Revisions
New	10-09-00	NA
A	10-16-00	Added category numbers and letters for item identification.
B	05-23-01	Added electrical panel marking and compressed gases categories.
C	03/15/02	Combined items 6A and 6D. Deleted item 10B, 12B, 12C, and 15D due to redundancy.

FIGURE 5.2   Part 4.

STANDARD WORK, VISUAL SYSTEMS, AND TPM

Standard Work. Developing standard work is a key element in the implementation of lean methodologies. Writing the standards for 5S organization in each area and assigning responsibilities for maintaining the standards are the first steps toward implementing standardized work. The unannounced audits monitor and provide an incentive to maintain the gains. Audits, though, would be a waste of time and effort if the standards for 5S were not in place and being practiced daily.

When a non-conformance occurs in a work area, the approach toward developing standard work is outlined below:

1. Ask whether the process or specification was well-documented. If the answer is, "No," then the documentation will be written or corrected as needed. Everyone is then trained on the new document(s).
2. If the process was well-documented and communicated, then the manager must decide whether retraining or discipline is appropriate for the non-conformance.

This process ensures that the standardization of the workplace is continually expanded and improved. When a better way is discovered, the documentation is changed, training occurs, and the operational benefits start the next day. This illustrates how standardized work can not only sustain the improvements but also provide a platform for continuous improvement.

Visual Systems. When the 5S system was initially implemented, eliminating unneeded tools and other material was part of the first S, Sort. The Second S, Set In Order, involved labeling drawers, organizing supply inventories, and creating shadow boards for housekeeping tools. This is a simple, systematic way of identifying a place for everything needed in a work area. Some work groups even identify the location of the wall clock with a label that says, "Clock." Any unneeded tools were removed from the area as there is no longer an assigned place for them. Another side benefit of these visual systems is training new associates becomes much easier and more effective.

As part of the certification standard, bulletin boards are also placed in each area. These bulletin boards include before and after pictures of the area, 5S audit scores, and a standard work area map. Over time, this bulletin board has led to posting daily and monthly productivity and quality performances, shipment performances, and other operational data. This information is current and is part of the visual systems program of plant management.

Total Productive Maintenance (TPM). Monroe's TPM program was implemented in 2004 and is still in the process of growing into other areas of the company. The disciplined work habits learned in the 5S process help expedite the TPM process. For this reason, all work areas become 5S-certified before chartering an organized TPM team.

SUMMARY

The 5S process that began at DNA's Monroe site in 1999 continues to be the foundation for continuous improvement. This process helped facilitate a cultural shift and the teamwork required for the journey to world class. With 5S as their foundation, the sky is the limit for Deceuninck North America's world-class initiatives.

QUESTIONS

- Do you have a 5S program? Is it focused on more than just organizing and cleaning work areas?
- Are your work areas audited and certified to ensure they comply with 5S guidelines? Do you have unannounced audits?
- Is success or failure in maintaining 5S certification tied to performance reviews?
- Are employees empowered as a result of your 5S program?
- Is standard work tied to your 5S efforts?

Cash Powell Jr. is associate director, University of Dayton Center for Competitive Change. He is a member of the editorial board of *Target*, and a member of the board of directors of the Dayton APICS Chapter.

Steve Hoekzema is Director of Operations at Deceuninck North America's extrusion plant in Monroe, OH.

Note

1. Effective January 1, 2005, Dayton Technologies' Monroe facility officially changed its name to Deceuninck North America (DNA). This change is a result of the purchase of former industry competitor, Vinyl Building Products, which has facilities in Little Rock, AR and Oakland, NJ. These Deceuninck facilities have supplied high-quality extrusions to vinyl window and door fabricators across North America for more than 35 years. Deceuninck Group, located in Belgium, is the parent company of Deceuninck. They are a worldwide leading manufacturer of vinyl window systems and profiles for the construction industry, operating 23 subsidiaries, both production and sales, throughout Europe, North America, and Asia.

6

Team-Centered, Continuing Improvements at General Dynamics Advanced Information Systems: Teamwork and a long-term commitment to continuous improvement make the difference

Jim Tennessen and Lea A.P. Tonkin

IN BRIEF

Employees at the General Dynamics Advanced Information Systems operation in Bloomington, MN have been committed to continuous improvmenet since the late 1980s. They use a two-tier teamwork approach as well as lean and Six Sigma concepts to achieve higher performance in quality and other key metrics, as they shared during a recent AME educational event.

Well on their way to organization-wide high performance through continuous improvement (CI) practices, people at the General Dynamics Advanced Information Systems operation in Bloomington, MN (see the box, "About General Dynamics Advanced Information Sustems") shared some of their "lessons learned" in an AME workshop. During the "Creating a Culture of Continuous Improvement" event, they described how their people-focused teamwork has led to performance gains such as work-in-process reductions, cycle time reductions, and quality improvements.

IMPROVEMENT HISTORY

The organization's CI journey has roots in the late 1980s when they began using their first continuous flow lines. They've since added several more continuous improvement tools reflecting lean and Six Sigma concepts. "We have taken the best of both approaches and rolled them into an overall approach of continuous improvement," said Brian Schubloom, senior manager, manufacturing.

"The key to our CI success has been our people," Schubloom continued. "We use a team approach to CI, where every employee has an opportunity and, in fact, an expectation to participate. Metric-driven CI has become very much a part of our culture." (See Figure 6.1.)

Brian Schubloom explained that they use two different types of CI teams, the permanent factory team and the temporary kaizen teams. "These teams are the backbone of our CI efforts," he said. "They are what make our efforts to constantly improve our products and processes continuous, and indeed a part of our culture."

The factory team concentrates on those CI activities related to quality improvement and cycle time reductions within their areas. When improvement challenges are beyond the scope of the factory teams, a kaizen team is formed. They may address projects such as 5S, Value Stream Mapping (VSM), and Six Sigma.

"Each type of CI team has its own pros and cons. We have achieved outstanding results by using both approaches together," said Schubloom.

ABOUT GENERAL DYNAMICS ADVANCED INFORMATION SYSTEMS

General Dynamics Advanced Information Systems, headquartered in Arlington, VA, is a leading provider of transformational mission solutions in command, control, communications, computers, intelligence, surveillance, and reconnaissance (C4ISR). The operation in Bloomington, MN, focuses on ruggedized network centric computing hardware and software for the tactical ISR arena. The systems are deployed on a wide range of airborne, ground, sea, and space-based military platforms.

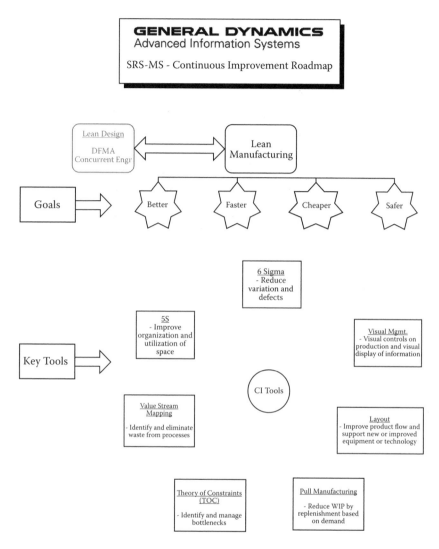

FIGURE 6.1 Tool kit for lean improvements.

PERMANENT TEAMS — FACTORY TEAMS

General Dynamics' Minnesota manufacturing operation produces rugged, high-reliability electronics in a low-volume, high-mix model environment. Therefore, the production floor is divided into factory teams rather than organized according to product lines (not enough repetitive volume). Employees perform a similar type of manufacturing operation on a wide

FIGURE 6.2 Employees discuss metrics and issues requiring problem-solving activities during daily stand-up meetings.

variety of products assigned to their team. Each factory team consists of production employees, a team lead, a planner, and a support engineer.

Each factory team has its own factory team center which is a communication board where information is posted by and for the employees. The factory team center contains information about production metrics related to quality and scheduling information, said Schubloom.

All of the production employees of a factory team have a daily stand-up meeting at the factory team center to review posted information and communicate about issues that could affect the team. They review the metrics, discuss key issues, and plan actions in their areas. The team members use problem-solving techniques to resolve issues affecting quality of the product, or on schedule delivery, etc.

In addition to the production employees, the lead, planner, and support engineer for the area attend the daily stand-up meetings. (A typical meeting is shown in Figure 6.2.) This communication is critical to the success of the factory teams. Direct support staff members are not an outside function, but are instead linked directly to the factory teams they support.

Whenever the team encounters the most critical issues — line down or shipment at risk — which can not be solved by the team, a "red flag" is raised to alert management of the need for assistance and they will address the issue during the daily factory walk, said Schubloom. The red flag, which is literally that, is posted at the appropriate factory team center board.

DAILY FACTORY WALK

The factory daily walk is just that, a walk of the entire factory completed by manufacturing management. "Put simply, the objective of the walk is to provide our manufacturing leadership with an understanding of all issues that affect quality and delivery of our products," Schubloom said. "We want our managers to be visible and accessible to facilitate communication of production issues. One of the members of the factory team is stationed at the team center board to communicate results and issues to the management team, and to answer any questions they might have. Again, the first step in CI is communication of the issues that require attention."

Quality and cycle time are the two main areas emphasized on the daily walk. Quality is analyzed using three different pieces of data: incoming defects, escaping defects, and internal defects per million opportunities (DPMO). During the factory walk, managers review performance in each of these areas.

DPMO measures internal quality that ultimately results in the calculation of a sigma level for each process center. "On a monthly basis, all of the sigma levels from various process centers are rolled into one, factory-wide sigma number. This number is communicated prominently within our business, and has been since the late 90s," Schubloom said. As discussed earlier, manufacturing management also discuss any red flag items and assign an "owner" to them during these meetings. Daily reviews of red flag items continue at the appropriate factory team centers until a corrective action is identified and implemented.

Cycle time data are also reviewed. "Our specific method for measuring cycle time is simply the number of units in WIP per day divided by the number of units delivered or exited from the factory. This calculation gives us a predictive indicator of schedule adherence and serves as a bottleneck identifier within our mixed model operation," stated Schubloom. More important than the raw number is the attention it brings factory centers that are running with high cycle times. The attention will help address the following questions: Do they need more resources? Is there a process or equipment problem? Is more or better training required? Is there a trend of increasing cycle time? If so, what can we do to reverse the trend before our customer is impacted?" Any negative trend or recurring problem can lead to initiation of a temporary kaizen team.

TEMPORARY TEAMS — KAIZEN

A kaizen team is formed when an identified issue requires focus beyond the scope of the daily factory team center meetings, said Schubloom. Recent examples include a 5S program initiative, a VSM event, implementation of a new visual management system, a setup reduction effort in circuit card automation, and a Six Sigma DMAIC (Define, Measure, Analyze, Improve, and Control) approach to variation reduction on a problematic process. To achieve a prompt solution, each of these issues required a focused approach, Schubloom said.

Once a kaizen opportunity has been identified, the executive continued, the first step is to determine who needs to be involved in the team. "All of the key stakeholders should be present, or at least have their organization represented. By stakeholders, I mean anyone who will be affected directly by the process that is being changed," stated Schubloom. "It's important to have this type of representation to both understand the current state process, and to improve 'buyin' on the future state process.

"We've had success with groups of five to eight people, but we've also recognized that the number is less important than having all relevant groups represented," he continued. "In other words — be flexible. If the problem that needs to be solved requires ten or 12 people, then include ten or 12 people. If the group size starts to become unmanageable, you may need to narrow the scope of your event. Perhaps you can have two separate events with a smaller number of participants."

Another key to the success of these teams is having an "outside set of eyes" in the kaizen events. "This person may be completely removed from the area that is being analyzed," said Schubloom. "There are times when those individuals who are closest to a process have a hard time seeing past their internal current state paradigm. What they end up doing is trying to find ways to make modest tweaks to the current state, when the real solution may be to tear the current state down to its foundation and start over. This is where some outside eyes can be helpful. They are often able to see that need, and the new process, more easily. In addition, this outside person doesn't have ownership of any piece of the process in question. This means that their suggestions, consciously or unconsciously, are not clouded by any self interest.

"We generally select a meeting facilitator before the kaizen events begin," Schubloom said. "This person is responsible for scheduling meetings, preparing an agenda, issuing minutes, etc. These meetings are often really brainstorming sessions more than structured meetings. The facilitator is critical in creating and maintaining an environment where creative thinking can take place. The facilitator also needs to work to involve all members of the team, even those who may be uncomfortable speaking in a group setting."

Mark Hulst, lean/CI leader, noted that many lessons have been learned during kaizen events. Some of the critical issues that have been important for the company include:

1. Determine how success will be measured at a kickoff meeting. What is the problem to be solved?
2. Avoid scope creep during your kaizen event. If brainstorming takes you to different areas than you anticipated, record the information and utilize a follow-up event if necessary.
3. Open, professional communication is needed during the meetings. Facilitators need to take responsibility to help make this happen.
4. The team succeeds or fails as a group.
5. The team is empowered to implement improvements. If you are a manager, don't organize a kaizen team whose purpose is just to come back with the solution that you have already decided you believe is the "right" solution. Be willing to be surprised by your team.
6. Have a closeout meeting where you review what's been done and document the plan going forward. Each open action must be assigned to a specific individual or small group.
7. Company leadership must show their appreciation for the work done by Kaizen teams (a method that is appropriate for your team and works with your company's policies). This is challenging work that often results in a huge impact to the company.

COMMUNICATION: VITAL LINK

"Even with the formation of factory teams, kaizen teams, factory team centers, and daily factory walks, we would see some limited continuous improvement throughout the factory without the communications between all teams and their members," said Schubloom. "If we stopped with communication only within a cell, we would be creating 'islands' of improvement within a factory team without understanding the interaction between individual processes and those up and down the product's value stream." The factory teams provide feedback to upstream processes and receive feedback from downstream processes.

Communication between teams is the key to the transformation of the factory team center into a tool for CI. Every factory team depends on feedback from downstream processes to validate their performance as an internal supplier. Similar feedback is also provided to upstream suppliers.

Six Sigma practitioners may refer to this relationship as "voice of the customer." "We view it as a fundamental piece of the CI puzzle," Schubloom said. "It forces each factory team to see their performance the way that their internal customer sees it. This daily communication is the critical step in our CI process. Before a problem can be solved, it must be identified. Frequently it is easier to complete this identification with the aid of feedback from downstream processes."

The standardized formatting of data and metrics throughout the factory serves two purposes. "First, it supports and simplifies cross-training initiatives, resulting in flexibility to handle spikes in demand in various factory teams," said Schubloom. "Second, it makes communication to the manufacturing management team via the daily walk much more straightforward."

To ensure that senior management is included in the communication link, the company has developed the Process Management Information System (PMIS) which collects data from the individual factory teams and rolls it up into departmental reports. The departmental reports are further rolled up into a total factory quality series of charts which are reviewed regularly by factory management.

THE JOURNEY CONTINUES

"When we first started measuring and reporting DPMO, we had an initial goal of achieving 3.0 sigma. Now, after nearly a decade using this methodology, we were able to end 2004 with a 12-month rolling average of nearly 5.3 sigma," Brian Schubloom said. "This is significant because each tenth of a sigma — for instance 5.2 to 5.3 — is a 30 percent quality improvement increase. For us to go from 3.0 to 5.3 sigma took 20 levels of 30 percent improvements. Our goal this year is to achieve better than ten percent continuous improvement, and we are on target to do just that.

"The three-step process of gathering, reviewing, and acting on data has been repeated over and over again to help us reach this level of performance," he stated. "We use both temporary and permanent teams to provide this data, and to provide the expertise on how to make improvements. These teams, and more specifically the people who serve on them, are what has made our continuous improvement journey a success."

QUESTIONS

- Does every one of your employees have not only an opportunity but an expectation to participate in continuous improvement efforts?
- Do you have both permanent teams and temporary teams?
- Does management walk your factory floor every day?
- Do you have strong, ongoing communication among all teams and employees?

Jim Tennessen of Tennessen Associates, Inc., is based in Minneapolis, MN and is the AME North Central Region president.

Lea A.P. Tonkin, Woodstock, IL is the editor of *Target*.

7

Re-Making Furniture Making at Hickory Chair Company: Their "secret weapon": employees

Deborah Porto and Michael Smith, PhD

IN BRIEF

Can a traditionally-managed furniture manufacturing business turn itself around to meet global competitors? How can a company's employees be engaged as a "secret weapon" to build critical performance improvements into a long-term cultural change process? This article reflects Hickory Chair Company's continuing journey to become a successful collaborative, team-based organization with laser focus on customer needs.

Imagine that you are "the sales guy" for an old business in an even older industry. Imagine that you have watched as many businesses in your industry have either gone bankrupt or taken their operations offshore.

Now imagine that the company president suffers a heart attack and dies suddenly. He knew about operations, and you have never worked in the plant at all, but you suddenly find yourself the new president. You begin to assess the situation, and quickly determine that the organization is in declining health. Sales are falling, and you know that something must be done. Your colleagues tell you that you cannot continue to make your product in the United States. Everyone knows that it can't be done here. Everyone is taking their production offshore. For you, such failure is not an option, but where will you find the resources and knowledge to make it work?

While you have only imagined this situation, we are describing the reality that faced Jay Reardon when he became president of Hickory Chair Company in Hickory, NC seven years ago. You will read how he discovered the resources within himself and the employees to not only turn the company around, but also enable the company to keep operating in the United States. Jay Reardon has expressed his desire to contribute to success in other organizations in agreeing to share his experience and access to the people and operations at Hickory Chair with us, so that we can describe what we found to the readers of *Target*.

THE REALITY

The improvement path has been long and difficult, but profits are up significantly. Sales in 2005 were 14 percent higher than in the previous year, and delivery times are down to between 14 and 21 days from six to eight weeks. Savings from improved business processes have meant that in spite of rapidly-increasing prices for materials and services that Hickory Chair purchases, they have not had to increase prices in more than four years.

The success at Hickory Chair contrasts sharply with the general performance of the furniture industry. The news in North Carolina, traditionally one of the major centers for furniture manufacturing, has been full of stories about plant closings and layoffs in the furniture industry. As awareness of the changes at Hickory Chair has spread, it has created a buzz among furniture companies and other manufacturers. We have repeatedly been asked, "What is happening over there?"

Jay Reardon explains that the company is doing EDGE (Employees Dedicated to Growth and Excellence; see the box, "Employees Dedicated to Growth and Excellence [EDGE]"). He continues that it is not the popular "lean manufacturing" or the renowned Toyota Production System (TPS). Instead, "It is the Hickory Chair business system," he said. "It is a business system that engages employees to make their work safer and easier so that our customers can be sitting comfortably in their chair or sofa they order in their house." Related performance improvements include shorter cycle times, reduced waste, higher quality, and faster product shipment. (See employees in various work areas in Figures 7.1, 7.2, 7.3 and 7.4.)

HICKORY CHAIR, A BRIEF HISTORY

In 1911 the Surry Chair Company was purchased by a group of investors and relocated to Hickory, NC where it became the Hickory Chair Manufacturing Company. The Surry Chair Company's motto was "Chairs Made Better Than Seems Necessary." The new company adopted this philosophy and expanded the assortment quickly from just dining chairs to all types of chairs, rocking chairs, and sofas. It became the first residential upholstery manufacturer based in Hickory.

The Hickory Chair Manufacturing Company merged with two other companies, Martin Manufacturing Company and the Hickory Furniture Company during the Depression, their combined strength enabling prosperity during this difficult period. The Hickory Chair Manufacturing Company also pioneered the marketing of reproduction furniture during the 1930s. After an antique English spool bed was found in the home of Dorothy Robinson, a descendant of Henry Weidner, the first settler in the Catawba Valley, the company developed the successful Dorothy Robinson collection with this bed and an accompanying suite of furniture. Its tradition of antique reproductions and adaptations had begun.

During World War II, most furniture manufacturing was eliminated to support war efforts. In 1941, the Hickory Chair Manufacturing Company negotiated for the rights to manufacture and market reproduction furniture under the James River Plantation license. Plantations along the James River in Virginia, the homes of early presidents and other prominent families, were filled with fine 18th century furnishings. Although the collection was not manufactured until 1943 because of war restriction, it became the oldest and largest collection of 18th century mahogany reproductions in America.

After the war ended, Hickory Furniture and Martin Manufacturing became Hickory Manufacturing Company and the Hickory Chair Manufacturing Company became Hickory Chair Company. Hickory Chair Company manufactured dining chairs and upholstery and purchased its James River Collection wood products from the Hickory Manufacturing Company. This relationship continued until 1967 when the Lane Company purchased Hickory Chair Company.

Hickory Chair reissued the James River Collection to celebrate its 50th anniversary in 1961. Mrs. John F. Kennedy's announcement in 1962 that the White House had undergone a massive restoration and that period furnishings would be acquired to return the historical appearance of its rooms spurred demand for antique reproductions.

The Lane Company began manufacturing the James River Collection for Hickory Chair Company in 1968. In 1982, Hickory Chair opened a wood products factory to manufacture its own case goods (helping the company to improve quality and expand its offerings beyond the James River Collection).

Hickory Chair Company facilities (factories, warehouse, office, and showroom) encompass nearly one million square feet. Located in Hickory, NC, the company is now owned by Furniture Brands International (the largest furniture corporation in the world, publicly traded as FBN).

Hickory Chair has a staff of over 450 non-union skilled craftsmen. Its product selection ranges from 18th century mahogany reproductions to Romantic furnishings and casual furnishings in addition to designer collections by Thomas O'Brien, Mariette Himes Gomez, and Alexa Hampton.

Note: This description is drawn from the company's website www. hickorychair.com where additional company information and its products can be viewed.

While Hickory Chair's success in the face of substantial bad news would appear to present unbridled opportunity, such industrial decline presents challenges, even for the remaining successful firms. As furniture manufacturing has moved offshore, Hickory Chair has become concerned that they may not be able to continue obtaining the high-end metal hardware that represents an important contribution to the perceived value of their furniture from local suppliers. When the market constricts, important suppliers face critical business challenges, and this is but one of many trials that may face successful companies in declining industries. For Hickory Chair, and others in similar positions, there is need for a healthy manufacturing sector and vitality in their respective industries in order for them to sustain their success (one reason for sharing on the part of successful organizations).

EMPLOYEES DEDICATED TO GROWTH AND EXCELLENCE (EDGE)

Originally EDGE was a program:

- Employees were asked to identify problems
- The EDGE Steering Committee determined the priority of the problems to fix
- EDGE teams were created and they found root causes and proposed solutions
- The EDGE Steering Committee determined what suggestions would be implemented
- Employees applied tools such as Kanban.

Managers as well as all employees learned from experience and had a key realization:

- People are the most valuable component
- Only people are capable of learning, creating, and problem solving
- Only people are limitless.

Today EDGE is:

- Attitude, a way of thinking, constant change for the better
- Organizational change
- Development of a culture that continuously improves everywhere, everyday
- Creating an environment that strives to make every process the most efficient work flow considering safety, quality, quantity, and cost
- Culture focused on the customer first — both internal and external
- Factory and office applications
- Next person in line is the customer
- The supplier adds value
- The dealer adds value.

EDGE teams:

- Use data to focus on the real cause of a problem and make the best decision
- Ask directly for employee ideas

FIGURE 7.1 Vance Snyder, a Hickory Chair Company carver.

FIGURE 7.2 Finish operation; Bobby Michael is shown.

TAKING A CLOSER LOOK

We decided to document their improvement because changes in how they work and think have led to outstanding performance. The challenges that Hickory Chair has surmounted are starkly evident in that the furniture manufacturing industry has drastically reduced manufacturing capacity

FIGURE 7.3   Hand-painting furniture; pictured is Lynn Killian.

FIGURE 7.4   Johnny Davis in the spring operation.

in the United States during the seven-year period that has seen Hickory Chair's resurgence. (See the box, "Industry Context of Improvement at Hickory Chair Company.")

We sought to understand how and why Hickory Chair had such performance improvement while others in the industry retreated and hunted for solutions based upon cheap labor in other countries. This article represents our synthesis of some of the reasons for their success, presented in the hope that it might help to embolden other manufacturers, above all other furniture operations, to take the steps necessary to successfully improve the performance of their operations.

We expected "lean manufacturing" to be a part of the answer, but when we toured the manufacturing plant and talked with the employees we saw more than what we expected. At first we saw clean and color-coded work areas with orderly tools and materials. We saw well-organized wood, frames, sewing, and upholstery work areas with squares painted on the floor indicating what and how much should be there. More extensive study revealed that the reasons for success lay deeper than these first impressions. Success was not rooted in the tools and techniques of lean manufacturing, as such. When we looked closer we saw people laughing, talking to each other, and teams working on improving their processes. The inanimate objects we saw at first are what many people understand "lean" to be. However, those inanimate objects are really just the result of the spirit and drive among employees to improve how things are done at Hickory Chair. So we wondered if they aren't doing "lean," what are they doing? This is what we set out to understand and share with other organizations.

The term "lean" was coined to describe the physical processes researchers observed at Toyota.[1] TPS, a system combining philosophy, management, and people, has been written about extensively,[2] but it has not been applied as successfully at other companies. A large industry of consultants has developed to provide their interpretation and experience of lean, for a fee. We believe that Hickory Chair has captured the spirit of TPS, not simply applied lean tools.

Hickory Chair's initial attempt at implementing lean was to hire an outside consultant. The consultant did some process mapping and told management what improvement steps were needed. He did not explain to the production employees what he was doing or how he was doing it. When the consultant left, a newly-hired supervisor who had experience with lean manufacturing started working with employee teams on improvement projects and training all employees on the basic concepts behind EDGE. The early results were small spot improvements, but the results grew as more and more employees were involved.

Hickory Chair made the critical realization that organizational change was needed and that without this change, "lean tools" would not work. Reardon insisted that managers must first change from a traditional top-down management style and instead act as leaders, coaches, and supporters.

INDUSTRY CONTEXT OF IMPROVEMENT
AT HICKORY CHAIR COMPANY

Hickory Chair Company is part of an industry that has long been an important part of the economy in North Carolina. Data from the Employment Security Commission of North Carolina (ESC) indicate that employment in the type of furniture manufacturing conducted by Hickory Chair accounted for approximately seven percent of manufacturing employment in the state in 2000.

In recent times, furniture manufacturing has increasingly been sacrificed to furniture importing, so that Hickory Chair's success as described in the article is notable at a time when the industry and manufacturing generally have fared poorly. Based upon employment data available from the ESC, in 1990 there were 69,580 people employed in manufacturing household/institutional furniture in North Carolina. By 1997, the year in which Jay Reardon became president of Hickory Chair, there were 58,544 people employed in such manufacturing, a decrease of 11,036, or 15.9 percent in employment. Between 1997 and the first quarter of 2005, employment in manufacturing household/institutional furniture saw an additional loss of 15,637 jobs, a decline of 26.7 percent relative to employment for 1997, and a cumulative reduction since 1990 of 38.3 percent. This loss in employment in furniture manufacturing has taken place against the backdrop of tremendous losses in manufacturing employment overall, down by 229,616 jobs between 1997 and the first quarter of 2005 in North Carolina, according to ESC data.

Improvement momentum did not increase until a high degree of employee involvement was achieved. The new outlook required persistence and a willingness to learn from trial and error, fed by enthusiasm for improvement. The focus would be on "what we should do" instead of "what we can do."

One method for comparing the essence of what Hickory Chair is doing compared to various "lean manufacturers" is to put what you see and hear through a people filter. Pour all the activities, reports, and projects through the filter and only actions involving people pass through. At Hickory Chair, most of what they do would pass through. Actions that involve people are what make the difference here.

Originally, EDGE was a program where formal teams were chartered by an EDGE steering committee. However, the management team came to realize that this formal structure limited the implementation of new ideas for improvement. As the organization took ownership of the concepts and processes, EDGE became more of a philosophy of values and how work was done, driven by employee concerns than a standard process. Today there is formal chartering of teams when issues and anticipated changes extend cross-functionally. Control for changes within departments rests with the departments, and such teams may consist of just several employees directly involved with the immediate issue. Finally, the least formality exists at the level of changes in processes at the personal level, which are dealt with individually in many cases.

Today, many formal teams actually function primarily to train the next group of team leaders, who in turn enter their work areas to implement the more informal processes described here. Reardon notes that by removing a top-heavy controlling system, Hickory Chair is now able to see continual improvement occurring all over the organization at a rapid pace. Creativity cannot be controlled into existence, and with the release from control, all the members of the organization are positioned to contribute innovation. The key to avoiding chaos, according to Reardon, is that respect must be present throughout the organization. Thus, an individual or team that is considering a change in a process that may affect others will consult those potentially affected as a matter of respect. The employees, as we describe below, have translated this respect into consideration of other employees as neighbors.

WHAT WE OBSERVED: THE ROLE OF LEADERSHIP

Both the criteria for the Shingo Prize and Malcolm Baldrige National Quality Award Program Criteria for Performance Excellence place heavy emphasis on the role of organizational leadership in initiating and sustaining organizational excellence. From this perspective, it was clear that we needed to explore the role of leadership in the transformation at Hickory Chair Company. What we found was that Jay Reardon displayed an awe-inspiring degree of intensity and focus on sustaining and improving his company (and the furniture industry), while serving his customers and employees. Our experience with Reardon suggests that he is a sensitive, intuitive, and driven individual with a high moral code. In our interviews, we found sources of his driven approach to his work and life in his sense of right and wrong, and of responsibility to family, employees, and the community. He talked about the importance of respecting local mores, a potential source of his concern about doing things in ways that were both right in a broad sense and correct for his industry, his community, and his company. As will be illustrated by examples presented later in this article, everyone from senior management to employees in all functional areas continue to build leadership skills.

Before becoming company president, Reardon was a self described, "sales guy" and did not know what to do in manufacturing. As the new president, he did two very important things: 1) He asked employees for help and 2) he started experimenting with different improvement ideas.

Reardon read articles and books about what other successful companies were doing to improve, and noticed that many of those companies mentioned work based on TPS. He sought out and met Hajime Ohba and his team at TSSC, Inc. (originally the Toyota Supplier Support Center, information available at www.tssc.com). Ohba is known and respected worldwide for his efforts to assist organizations where the leadership is prepared and willing to learn about TPS and apply TPS principles to their own situation, a description that readily fit Reardon. In Ohba, Reardon found an advisor who generously provided help and advice, enhancing improvement work at Hickory Chair.

However, in our study, we found consistent evidence that the team at Hickory Chair did not simply adopt external methods or wait to be told what to do. Instead, they learned by trying and experimenting. They did not implement TPS, but developed their own approach, assisted along the way by the pointers, experience, and road signs offered by TPS, as presented by Ohba.

One indicator of this personalization is that Hickory Chair employees developed EDGE as their method for engaging employees in continuously making their work safer and easier. Orientation materials for new employees point out that when all employees adopt and use EDGE principles (such as being an active participant in identifying and solving problems in their work areas), they continually develop new ways for making furniture so customers benefit by receiving their furniture order, customized to personal preferences, in less time. We found that the Hickory Chair business system brings a clear focus to meeting customer needs and desires more quickly, at lower cost by making work safer and easier for the employees.

EDGE-inspired results are evident in both the administrative and manufacturing areas. Customer service employees, for example, identified their problem of not always having information to answer customers' questions. The lack of information meant that they had to research the requested material and then call the customer back, which slowed down the customer's order. To improve this process, customer service employee training was enhanced, so that these employees now answer 94 percent of customers' questions during the first call.

Another example of the EDGE process is in the finishing area where the final stain is applied to the wood. Changing from one finish to another involved cleaning, loading, and resetting the finishing equipment. An employee in the area had the idea that the finish area should be like a soda fountain where the finish, like Coke or Dr. Pepper beverages, were always available at the touch of a button. The finishing area was rearranged so that the common finishes were always available and no changeover was required. This modification helped to bring the work in process (WIP) inventory down and allowed more flexible color options.

The multiple floors of the manufacturing plant present challenges to communication and product flow. Furniture frames are assembled on the floor below the upholstery area, and initially there was limited communication between the two departments, resulting in hundreds of wooden frames sent up to upholstery staging and manufacturing areas. The frames were scattered in large bunches, cluttering the upholstery area. An EDGE team identified this as a problem to implementing sequencing and created a simple signal to request the next frame, pulling a string that turned on a light bulb overhead the upholstery station making the request and in the staging area, indicating that another frame was needed. A material handler looks for the light, retrieves the next frame, and puts it in a designated area in front of the lighted upholstery employee's work area. The employees emphasized that in this example, it isn't the light that is important, but the process that was invented.

The EDGE process is not limited to employees inside the company. Hickory Chair dealers are invited to attend the "Hickory Chair University" at the manufacturing plant. At the one-day session, the dealers meet the management team and supervisors, learn about the company philosophy, meet the employees, and observe how the furniture is made. Before the factory tour, the tour guide invites the group to participate in helping Hickory Chair attain the national safety record for the furniture industry by wearing safety glasses. Hickory Chair takes this opportunity to ask the dealers directly, "What is your dream of how Hickory Chair could double your business?" Responses at the session we attended included providing larger stained finish samples to better see the stain color, a brochure to explain why veneer is more ecological than solid wood, design and offer more small occasional tables, and make a video to show end customers how the furniture is made to emphasize the craftsmanship of furniture built in the United States. The dealers discussed what impressed them after the factory tour. They mentioned that Hickory Chair was minimizing lot sizes to increase volume (different from competitors), the simplicity of light signals versus computerized scheduling, the courage to give employees the freedom to make improvements, the fact that quality is enhanced at every work station rather than at the end of the line, and the impression that no one in Hickory Chair would ever say in response to a problem, "That is not my job." The dealers also expressed the idea that what they observed at Hickory Chair would encourage other furniture manufacturers not to give up on manufacturing in the United States. At the end of the day, Reardon summed up the company philosophy to the dealers as, "Believe in your heart the potential of your employees and you will achieve great things from your employees."

In the next section, we look at how an organization can initiate change like what we have seen at Hickory Chair. In particular, we examine the extent to which leadership involvement is necessary for organizational transformation, and the essential elements of such leadership for substantial sustainable transformation that yields new levels of organizational performance.

LEARNING TO LEAD MORE SUCCESSFULLY

Jay Reardon and his team have been working at transforming Hickory Chair for seven years. Our observations suggest that part of what makes the company stand apart from less successful organizational transformations, and lean transformations in particular, is the type and style of leadership in the organization. It appears that the commitment to improvement and disciplined focus on the customers and employees is more important to success than are the exact actions or their timing. Leadership needs to maintain and communicate a sustained desire to attain a clearly-defined organizational future. They also must intensely focus on the human relationships at the heart of the organization. Although there is no roadmap for success in remaking your organization, there are things that you can learn to help you lead your organization more successfully.

Whatever personal attributes Reardon brings to his role, for example, he would not be effective without *leading in a fashion that is genuine and unique to him and his situation.* Reardon's early experiences helped to form his leadership style. He may also have personality elements that provide a good foundation for leading in the way that we have observed. Our description of what has worked for Reardon at Hickory Chair does not represent a recipe to be followed, but instead suggests that other leaders fashion their own unique recipe for leadership. This leaves room for you, the reader, to shape your own means to lead and implement improvements. In fact, your leadership cannot be genuine without your unique leadership formula.

Caring about people, getting them involved, and seeking ways to make their lives better is another central focus of Reardon's conversations and activities. Reardon often notes that people skills and communication skills are extremely important to the transformation of Hickory Chair, yet these skills are not adequate to accomplish the transformation. Instead, they must be genuinely applied to get people involved. This is an area where your background may make a difference in how easily this comes to you, but most people can work to develop better connections with people (in this case, particularly with employees and customers).

Effective connections with internal and external customers are critical. The best sales people can all tell stories about the lives of their best customers and what is important in the lives of those customers. Reardon readily recognizes the importance of connecting with and meeting the genuine needs of customers, but the same personal focus that helps him in the sales role also helps with his employees, the internal customers. Early in his career, he was an insurance adjuster. He recounted how at one point a family lost their pickup truck in an accident that also severely injured the daughter. The father wanted a new truck, but Reardon could see that the daughter was going to need extensive cosmetic surgery and medical care. His supervisor told him to settle for the new truck and nominal personal injury — a lower personal standard that led Reardon to a career change, and employment at Milliken.

At 27 years of age, Reardon became a driver at the Furniture Market for Mr. Milliken. In this role, he learned a great deal about how Milliken did business, and also added to his listening skills. *He learned to have confidence in people, and look to them for knowledge about how to make things better.* He also learned about how some people are mavericks, while others are trouble makers. In Reardon's description, the maverick does things differently, but without pushing too far. By contrast, the trouble maker may undertake similar actions, but fails to observe the limits of organizational and interpersonal tolerance. Thus, the maverick, as portrayed by Reardon, is successful in promoting change, where the trouble maker is viewed as an organizational pariah, which he sees as causing to be ineffective in implementing change. Reardon later moved into the furniture business and eventually became the vice president of sales at Hickory Chair. When he was suddenly promoted to president, he realized he had a great deal to learn, so he called people within the organization together and listened to what they had to say. This approach set the tone for what was expected from the management team.

Looking to a broad range of sources for information also works well. As he began to work to develop his role with Hickory Chair management, Reardon instituted a reading program, finding books and readings that seemed to carry an important message for the business, and asking the management team to read and discuss the readings. In retrospect, not all of the readings pointed in the right direction, but the program served to emphasize a requirement for a sustained effort to find new ways to orchestrate the organization's work, and to underscore mastery of new thinking as a focus for the management team and the entire organization.

Reardon readily addresses the importance of *changing the style that many managers initially utilized in approaching implementation of new ways of doing work* at Hickory Chair. All managers, including Reardon, participated in 13 weeks of team-building training. He somberly admits that this effort was only partially successful. Underscoring the challenge of changing long-standing approaches, he noted that as more collaborative practices evolved, the company turned over about 70 percent of the managers. Among the turnovers at Hickory Chair were two vice presidents who set up battles between workers. Reardon initially tried to work with them, but eventually both of them retired. The human resources director also indicated an inability to make the necessary changes.

Such turnover is sobering, yet it is in keeping with experiences reported in other successful transformations. While the approach was different when Toyota and GM formed NUMMI, given that a termination and re-hiring process was utilized, 85 percent of the hourly employees from the old GM-Fremont plant were re-hired and almost none of the salaried employees were re-hired.[3] The evidence available suggests that the style and personality of the managers are critical to successful transformation.

While we believe that it is possible for anyone to *develop greater sensitivity to those with whom they are working*, a critical point is that such a change can only occur when the individual is genuinely committed to making such a change. Some people initially want to do so, and others may be willing to be led into non-traditional ways, but where managers actively resist such changes, termination may be the only practical approach. The central concern is that without leadership expressed through a management team displaying genuine concern for the employees of an organization, progress will be significantly hampered.

Reardon pointed to the *involvement of employees* as vital to successful organizational improvement. As noted above, their contributions are only leveraged when the proper management philosophy is present. One index of such presence can be seen in employee turnover. About four years ago at Hickory Chair, turnover was about 13 percent. Last year it was seven percent, of which voluntary turnover was about two-three percent. The difference is accounted for in part by a no-smoking policy that drove a number of people away, but this is seen as a safety issue.

We found it exciting to witness Reardon and other managers' connection to the employees. We saw it when they stopped and talked with employees and joked with them about getting the visitors to sell more furniture. Noting that respect can also be reflected through genuine interest in employees, wanting to know, "What is their story?" Reardon expressed disappointment when other corporate leaders seem unable to uncover the value in their employees. In this context, *the lesson with the greatest value is that your success is not dependent upon some magic ingredient from outside, but instead springs from recognizing the worth of those already in your employ.* Recognizing their value and communicating that their input is valued rests at the very heart of your success, but unless the message is heart-felt, do not expect it to take hold. The leader must be able to tell a new story, but the story that you tell must include the story of the people upon whom your success will depend.

SUSTAINING THE IMPROVEMENT MOMENTUM

To sustain improvement, Reardon and other managers needed to create an atmosphere of positive tension to keep a routine and pace of improvement. While they can describe the performance of the organization in terms of traditional data, we found that they also described decisions as being informed by walking the factory floor and visiting with customers. Intuition derived from contact with the work, workers, and customers was described as critical in establishing improvement targets, such as new goals for leadtimes.

Reardon noted that intuition (in addition to more routine measures) allowed him to take a more holistic sense of the system into account. That holistic perspective might be utilized to determine the extent to which the system could realistically be expected to improve some measured value, however. Another attribute ascribed to intuition was sensitivity to current situations; that is, "having your antennas up all the time" — to address individual concerns while looking to do the right things for those affected by the system.

Among the right things Reardon described is that we should be manufacturing in the United States: "We owe it to ourselves to make things here." He hates it when someone gives up, such as when organizations chase low labor costs. There is no end to cheap labor, he said. For example, furniture manufacturing has moved from Michigan to North Carolina, to Mississippi, to Mexico, and now to Asia in pursuit of low costs. "Can't we think of a better way?" he asks. "Can't we stay close to the market?" He explains that by being both close and responsive to customers, manufacturing at home is an opportunity.

The spirit behind attempts at organizational change directly affects their level of sustained success, Reardon believes. Successful application of TPS concepts, for example, depends on an underlying spirit. As an example, if you are asking, "Why did I have to do those sit-ups?" after leaving your personal trainer, you probably did not get the fitness spirit, and only a list of things to do.

Likewise, the manager who directs that lean tools be utilized has missed the essential point. Those who grasp the underlying philosophy focus on improving the working environment of employees. Reardon described the proper emphasis as shop floor well-being, making people feel part of the environment, not a tool. He observed that you can't embrace inanimate words such as quality, cost, and delivery — the buzzwords of lean. Employees and customers want a personalized environment that meets their needs. Walking through the workplace regularly and frequently, an offsite recognition dinner, and active participation in EDGE closeout meetings are among the ways that company leadership draws personal connections between what the company does and the employees.

PATH TO ENGAGEMENT OF EMPLOYEES: "REALLY CARING"

The path to engagement of employees has been supported by drawing on internal as well as outside resources. Although the management team had prided themselves on an employee focus, they decided to request a TPS facilitator from TSSC to work with the employees to enhance ongoing improvement activities. When the facilitator arrived, she introduced herself in a rather cursory manner, and proceeded directly to the plant floor. Although she was polite, her concern was the floor employees and their work at the point where value is added to the product by transforming wood, springs, and fabric or leather into chairs and couches.

Reardon noted that by her actions, the facilitator showed what, "Employees are our greatest resource" should mean. He learned that in spite of the management team's sense that they had made tremendous strides, they needed to learn the importance of a people focus in order to really improve their processes and improve customer satisfaction.

The TPS facilitator, for example, modeled people talk rather than talk about things. Her facilitation helped employees examine processes relative to the seven wastes (overproduction, waiting, transportation, the process itself, stock on hand, movement, and defective products)[4] characteristic of TPS-based approaches and how she could help them make their work easier on the floor. For instance, in looking at a process that added six cushions to a couch that required lifting, she asked why the people have to lift six pillows rather than about how the six pillows are added to the couch.

The facilitator also encouraged participation by having the team members present their work at the end of each project. Each team member was required to share what they had learned with members of the management team (not by merely putting up slides). The facilitator encouraged full discussion, so that each member got credit for what they learned.

The management team saw through her actions that the facilitator "really cares about people. She showed the total focus on people by living the example," Reardon said.

Not everyone who hears of such concern with the welfare of employees perceives it in positive terms. Some executives have condescendingly referred to the Hickory Chair approach as a "kumbaya" style. Reardon pointed out that caring about the employees does not mean that business performance is sacrificed. Without being financially viable we can't be socially responsible, he said, but social responsibility is the process measure to achieve the financial viability.

EMPLOYEE REACTION TO CHANGES

We now turn our attention to employee reaction to the changes. Change has become standard at Hickory Chair. Perhaps one of the most visible reminders of continuous change can be found in the transition of the former expediting room to a continuous improvement room where teams could have a quiet place to meet. The conversion was plain for the employees to see as they walked by the room's large glass window on their way into the plant each day. There was a clear message that the work in the room has gone from picking up where the system has failed to making things so they work correctly.

We interviewed a number of employees at Hickory Chair in completing our study, including both managers and line employees. We found that people throughout the organization felt very positively about changes, and were enthused about their personal roles, as well as about their personal assessments about the future for the company.

We had observed substantial advances in organizational performance ahead of formally beginning our interviews. Employees were involved in improving work processes as part of their personal daily activity in organizing their work areas; work area formal and informal teams working on exposed problems of standardized work; and EDGE teams working on cross-functional problems such as sequencing; and the company was reaping the benefits. However, shortly before we began our formal study, a new TPS facilitator helped the leadership at Hickory Chair take employee involvement to a new level, and our interviews reflect employee responses following this intervention. Our description will focus on interviews of some of the initial participants on teams that are being replicated rapidly throughout the organization.

The facilitator worked with the Hickory Chair employees to demonstrate the spirit of TPS — all employees are capable and responsible for problem identification and solving. She first walked the production floor and then selected a team of two men and two women from different areas of the plant — upstairs and downstairs (Hickory Chair is in an historic building with multiple floors). While the facilitator selected the team members, their supervisor, Steve Parkhurst selected a quality problem for the team to address.

The facilitator trained the team on the basics of waste identification and problem solving for one-and-a-half days. Her training material was simple — just a single sheet of paper with problem solving depicted as a funnel with inputs and outputs. She encouraged team members to see what was actually occurring in work processes and to discuss what they were witnessing.

The reader may want to compare this approach to the typical approach with large notebooks and extended training conducted in a formal classroom as part of many lean training programs. According to the employees who served on the EDGE team that worked with the TSSC facilitator, the facilitator immersed the team in work addressing real situations and had them base their work on personal observations. The focus was not on the impersonal, inanimate concept of waste, but forms of waste that created hard and awkward work (such as work that required lifting or bending) for people.

The team worked to solve the quality problem on the second day and presented their results on the third day to the senior management team. The presentation had many "before" and "after" pictures with explanations of the improvement on simple forms and an EDGE newspaper of follow-up items. The facilitator helped employees set up a problem-solving structure and expectations of employee roles, and also modeled a cadence of weekly problem solving. In the presentation on the work accomplished that week, each team member shared what they learned. The facilitator did not allow them to simply put up their slide in silence but encouraged them to discuss what they had learned. We found that the process modeled by the facilitator impressed the organizational leadership as a display of her sincere concern for the employees and energized the employees by engendering a sense of pride in their accomplishments. These themes are further elaborated in describing our discussions with several EDGE team members to learn more about their experience and reactions to the problem-solving teams.

Tim Causby was one of the four team members who initially worked with the TPS facilitator. He has worked at Hickory Chair for 23 years. A sense of pride in what had been accomplished was evident as Causby showed us the work of his team in resolving the initial quality problem. He said that what he was showing us was the work of the team, and that the facilitator encouraged and let the team have all the credit for their work.

The researchers, in examining what happened with this team, found that the situation differed significantly from what we have observed in some organizations where lean consulting groups are engaged. Often it appears in the final reports that the team is simply the supporting cast as the credit is claimed by the consultant.

Presentation skills, not often part of life for line employees, need to be developed in order for the team members to share their experiences. Causby described how the facilitator worked with the team to develop a presentation to management, and then required that each employee focus on describing what he or she had learned. While he said that this made him anxious, the presentation also helped him recognize that he could do something to fix problems, feel pride in his abilities, and motivate him to do it again.

Previously a team member, Causby next graduated to leading a team. He described how he modeled his experience with the facilitator by selecting his team members and getting another problem to work on from his supervisor. In addressing this problem, the team developed an approach that reduced the number of pieces of wood involved in a part where the upholstery meets the frame of a chair, improving the fit and appearance while simplifying production. This problem well illustrates the cross-functional nature of the projects the teams were tackling, involving workers from the wood and upholstery portions of the operations. From his perspective, Causby reported that the EDGE process and new teams were making a substantial difference in how he saw his work, since he was now involved in identifying problems and getting them fixed, instead of just writing problems down for someone else to fix and then seeing the problems ignored and forgotten. He noted that he would not want to return to previous ways of working. He particularly credited Reardon for bringing change to the organization, noting that "Jay is a real human. He is here even on Saturdays. He makes us feel good."

The theme of a nervous start on the team was echoed when we talked to another team member, Mike Farley, who was also a department manager. Farley noted that he overcame nervousness when he saw what the team accomplished. Farley told us that there were plenty of problems to keep any number of teams busy, if not in his area, then in other areas of the plant.

Another employee emphasized the importance of the philosophy, noting that at a previous employer, the approach was to get the product out, even if there were problems. He described how at Hickory Chair the EDGE process gave them a way to fix problems now and prevent them in the future, instead of fixing them later.

INCREASING BUY-IN, LOOKING OUT FOR YOUR NEIGHBORS

Danny Milam, who has worked at Hickory Chair for 12 years, told us that the EDGE teams' improvements led to increasing levels of interest and involvement from employees who had not previously supported change. He said the facilitator had promoted this new state by showing team members how to see waste. Milam reported his pleasure as others around him started seeing the waste. He had worked on a problem that resulted from a specification change that was not adequately communicated to all the parties who needed to respond to the change. He described shock in learning of this, and pleasure when the team's proposed solution was accepted. Milam noted that he could see the extent of the new philosophy at Hickory, noting that he did not feel enthusiasm for the problem-solving teams at first but that "seeing what I could do and that senior management listened" changed his mind. During his first team presentation, he said that he was sweating, "but senior managers listened to me and they took notes on what I said." At the end of the team's presentation, "Jay gave us the green light."

Milam's sense of what the teams are accomplishing shows in his assessment of where the company stands. He described Hickory Chair as the "top dog" in furniture, based on an assessment of his previous work experience and what he has heard from friends who work for other furniture manufacturers. He noted that Hickory Chair is promising short delivery times and doing it.

Milam echoed a theme that we previously identified in Hickory Chair's implementation of EDGE, when he described how continued improvements could be made if everyone just looked out for their neighbors. From his perspective, his neighbors were the departments before and after the area in which he worked, in contrast to a more typical approach the next process in line as a customer and the previous process as a supplier.

Paula Lowman has worked at the company for 26 years. She said that no one liked the changes at first. In the upholstery area, which had been paid on a piece rate (an incentive for rapidly producing good or bad parts), employees previously had been able to pick and choose work to maximize their money, but that had changed. She had not wanted to go to standard hourly pay, and working on items in order. She described herself as one of the most resistant to the change. However, she now acknowledged that quality suffered under the old system, and today she is an advocate for EDGE. She says that she could not return to working under the old philosophy, which she described as supporting a management approach captured in the phrase, "Keep your mouth shut and do your job." Her work with a team gave her a platform to go ahead and say things about her work area and processes that she had been thinking earlier.

Lowman told us that as she gained comfort with the EDGE process, and saw things improving, she realized that she could contribute to resolving long-standing problems. Now she is hearing from other workers about problems that they have, and realizing that these issues can be resolved, often by implementing relatively small changes (such as moving equipment or improving standardized work). Like others who we spoke with, she highlighted the work of teams across areas in the plant, noting that she now feels like she can look at how work from other areas impacts her work, and she can also participate in trying to address how work done in her area impacts others. She said that she has come to appreciate how a small issue in one area can result in large problems elsewhere, expressing the theme we heard earlier about employees needing to take care of their neighbors.

Lowman described improvements that had been made as making for a more pleasant and better organized workplace. For example, in the past,

FINANCIAL, OTHER PERFORMANCE IMPROVEMENTS

- Sales are increasing by double digits
- Profits are strong without any price increases in four years
- Inventories are one-half of what they used to be
- Inventory turns rose significantly
- Quality performance improved.

Jeff Anderson, the vice president of operations at Hickory Chair, said the indicators used to measure their business success are "safety, quality, customer service, and continuous improvement":

- Safety
  - Over seven million safe man hours, which is the industry record
  - Large decrease in the number of recordables (the number of times someone goes to the doctor)
- Quality
  - Significant decrease in returns and allowances as a percentage of sales
- Service
  - Parts bins 96 percent available
  - Fabric and leather 96 percent available
  - Upholstery cycle time of 14–21 days 96 percent of the time
  - Wood products delivery in two weeks or less 96 percent of the time
- Continuous Improvement
  - Setup reduction
  - Sequencing
  - Employee training.

The parent company, Furniture Brand, looks at revenue, cash flow, and return on investment across its different companies. Jeff Anderson points out that Hickory Chair's excellent financial performance is the result of achieving safety, quality, service, and continuous improvement goals.

He emphasized that Hickory Chair's business success is not from one area, but a combination of many efforts. He said, "The customer wants design, service, quality, and value. Hickory Chair is responding to what the customers want."

- Design — with new products made quickly with customization. With small batches so customer changes can be reflected in weeks rather than months.
- Service — continuously improving
- Quality — better than ever
- Value — no price increases in four years while at the same time design, service, and quality have improved.

"There will always be a place for furniture manufacturers in the United States that make customized products," said Anderson. "Some offshore furniture manufacturers have lower prices but not the quality and customization ability."

upholstery material was spread out and poorly organized. She said that now material is organized and grouped "like a family."

In addressing how she became an ardent supporter of the change efforts at Hickory Chair, Lowman attributed the shift to the effects of seeing positive changes, feeling appreciated, and seeing persistence in making things better. She contrasted such persistence with the past, when improvements would start and then fizzle out. Today, she believes that the company is headed in the right direction, and that she can see this change through better organizational communication. She told us that she feels that senior management consistently treats people with respect, and shares information, including financial information, both the good news and the bad news.

Like another employee interviewed in the upholstery area, Lowman expressed the wish that the people part of the changes had come earlier. From her perspective, leaders can motivate employees to join in change efforts by getting to know the people who work for the company, getting to know the product, and then showing the workers that they are willing to help make things better for all employees and customers.

ACCEPTING — AND QUESTIONING — CHANGE

Clearly, things at Hickory Chair are changing, but one manager was very concerned that we recognize that things are not perfect. In her words, "We've still got ugly babies." She added that there is "not a single day that goes by that we don't change something."

Dramatic change has been difficult for various people within the organization. For some managers, change from traditional ways does not work well with their personality or mental models of how work should be managed. In some cases a manager's inability to make the transition may require that they be moved out of the organization; in other cases the disconnect is not that extreme. In cases where there is enough movement toward accepting change, and the value that they contribute to the organization is great enough, disagreement may remain largely out of sight (although some individuals were willing to share their angst with outsiders). One manager we interviewed was not as optimistic as were the employees reported above, but he did acknowledge that Hickory Chair might not have remained in business without the EDGE-related changes.

Another indicator of the company's transition is in retrospective views of people who shifted their perspective. Many of the supervisors at Hickory Chair will now tell you that they can not imagine managing in another system. They have seen how much easier supervision is now, and would not like to return to the old ways of doing things. In our conversations with managers, we found that many of them were clearly imbued with this new spirit — evidence that the company's continuing improvement progress has gained broader acceptance.

As the transformation has progressed, the perspective on the need for external resources has changed. Initially, Hickory Chair relied on a number of "experts" hired from outside the firm. In some cases, these experts were recruited from firms where the transformation has proven far less durable than have the efforts at Hickory Chair. While these outsiders may have spurred movement in new directions, they brought with them a top-down approach to transformation. From the perspective of hindsight, Reardon can see the value that some of these outsiders brought to the early efforts, but he now recognizes the need to look internally to identify rising stars and start grooming them toward leadership.

Comparison of traits associated with effective transformation efforts contrasted with the traits associated with unsuccessful efforts.

Effective	Ineffective
Genuine, honest and open	Situation
Urgency, based upon legitimate concerns about the business	Any crisis will do; a new crisis every day
Believes in people	Searches for "better people"
Driven to improve things, sets and example	Directs change
Knows what things look great, there's more to be done	Proclaims success
Patient, but driven	A moving target
Knows that what matters is what the employees think	Looks to change behavior
Makes transformation unique to the organization	Implements programs
New thinking permeates the culture	Thinking is personality-dependent
Leverages assistance from outside to develop unique solutions; seeks alignment	Adopts approaches of outsiders – What's the next wave?
Customer-focused	Business results-focused
Delivers and sustained by results	Derailed in search of results

Once again, this dawning realization serves to highlight that while help from outside may be useful, the ultimate challenge is to create a system that nurtures nascent talent within the organization and fashions a path that is unique to your organization. There is the temptation to look toward apparent successes in other organizations. Yet leadership needs to question whether "outsiders'" contributions will be useful for their own organization and can withstand the test of time. Even if such examples are found, their leaders may not be well positioned to nurture the embryonic community of internal leadership that would be best positioned to fashion your unique path.

PRIDE, AND BELIEVING IN EMPLOYEES

While the methods of leadership may appear soft, and indeed, they rely on soft skills, the results are anything but soft. The changes at Hickory Chair have had profound impact on the business. Last year they did $62 million in business, and Reardon projects $70 million in the coming year. His question is, "When will Hickory Chair reach the goal of $100 million in revenue?"

Overall, a central theme is that of driving change by listening to people and helping them to figure out how to change things. In some ways, Jay Reardon is very much an orchestrator of a context in which others can engage in changing the system. Such organization-wide leadership emergence represents the only sustainable approach to fomenting continuous improvement for your organization.

For some people the role of the orchestrator may be more challenging than for others, but we have come to believe that most people, if driven by a genuine desire to change their own thinking and behavior, can make the changes necessary to lead successful organizational change.

TAPPING THE INTELLECTUAL CAPITAL OF EMPLOYEES

The feel of the Hickory Chair plant is different from many others where attention is drawn to the physical accomplishments like kanban cards and work cells. At Hickory Chair, our attention is drawn to the changes in people. The average tenure of employees is 10.5 years, so the majority of employees responsible for the transformation today are the same employees who worked in traditional ways. What has changed is the addition of a system that allows and encourages and respects the creativity of the employees. Hickory Chair's transformation is based on using the intellectual capital of their existing workforce.

Reardon expressed great concern that we should not over-state the role of his leadership in Hickory Chair's transformation, emphasizing that it is about the employees. He cautioned that charismatic leadership can be superficial (leaders either taking on the traits of a benevolent dictator or becoming a patronizing leader, expressing the belief that employees should be "involved," but only as long as the decision making stays with the managers). In some "lean" organizations, the departure of a charismatic leader reveals how all directives had been coming from the leader and the improvement responsibility had never been transferred to the employees.

Sometimes visitors to Hickory Chair remark about the company's successful transformation to a collaborative, employee-focused organization, adding that, "We can't get our people to do that." If they go back to their companies and discuss only the lean tools they had observed at Hickory Chair, they have overlooked and discounted the capability of their own people.

Hickory Chair employees told us how they felt about their role in the transformation. Their comments reflect the spirit of the company — a key to its success:

- Pride in their abilities, "seeing what I could do."
- Feeling that their ideas were important and appreciated. EDGE has given employees the opportunity to say what they had been thinking.
- Management needed and respected the employees. Management listened, took notes, walked the floor to see in person, and treated employees with respect.
- Optimism for the future of the company.
- Employees don't want to revert to the old way which was, "get the product out" and "keep your mouth shut and do your job."

A key accomplishment of Hickory Chair is capturing and developing the intellectual capital of the employees by developing a culture of respecting employees and giving them responsibility for identifying and solving their own work problems individually and in a team-based environment. The degree of employee responsibility and accomplishments, as well as their feeling of being respected by management and optimism for the future, make Hickory Chair employees shine. EDGE, as one employee said, "gave me the opportunity to say what I had been thinking … and to do something about it." That spirit is hard to see but easy to feel.

Hickory Chair boosted employee responsibility by making all employees salaried and providing them with cross training. Furniture manufacturing is one of the last industries to make the change to a salaried workforce. Jay Reardon noted that when Hickory Chair went to salaried pay instead of incentive pay, they learned that "incentive rates were cancerous to quality." Piece rates were a barrier to enlarging employees' responsibilities to improve their work conditions and processes. A salaried work force can accept more flexible work assignments, Reardon said.

The company chose to build upon the new-found flexibility by making sure that all employees were cross-trained to do multiple tasks in the completion of a particular component. In order to cross train, they developed visual and written standards for everything they make. The standards make variations and unusual conditions more visible so that employees can readily identify troublesome conditions and bring it to the attention of their supervisor or to their own EDGE team for improvement.

What has prevented most businesses from using the potential of their employees? What we learned from the example of Hickory Chair is that the senior manager's job is not problem solving but teaching, enabling, and encouraging employees to identify and solve their own problems.[5] By better leveraging the problem-solving capability of their employees, the company can begin to address problems throughout the organization. The potential of this multiplier effect, conservatively 12 problems identified and solved per employee per year initially, is huge. The improvement rate accelerates over time as each employee becomes more skilled at identifying and solving problems.

CONCLUSION

Hickory Chair Company is transforming the way it does business. They have made many successful financial and strategic decisions, but their ongoing success has been enabled by something much less tangible. The leadership has inspired the employees to believe in the future of the company and in their personal ability to contribute to that future. Hickory Chair has built a foundation of people whose ideals and values contribute to success in manufacturing furniture in the United States. These attributes are then directed toward positive change through universal involvement in an internally-developed process for problem identification and solving. But in spite of early success, everyone we met at the company recognized that success in the future depends on their working together to build upon and grow the foundation that they have established.

Jay Reardon, his staff, and employees have been aided in developing EDGE by their experience with TPS. They followed its spirit as they designed processes that were useful in making furniture. Jeff Liker writes in his book, *The Toyota Way*, about the spirit of TPS, "The more I have studied TPS and the Toyota Way, the more I understand that it is a system designed to provide the tools for people to continually improve their work. The Toyota Way means more dependence on people, not less. It is a culture even more than a set of efficiency and improvement techniques. You depend upon the workers to reduce inventory, identify hidden problems, and fix them. The workers have a sense of urgency, purpose, and teamwork ..."[6] This description applies to Hickory Chair and EDGE.

Much of the literature on how to implement lean manufacturing discusses tools and their application. The organizations most successful at transformation have designed tools that fit their specific needs and have not force-fit lean tools to all situations. The development, dissemination, and standardization of lean tools may be the visible portion of a lean transformation, but they are dependent on the more invisible foundation of establishing a culture among the organization's people to support new ways of thinking. We believe from our observations that this is Hickory Chair's unique accomplishment. They have developed a foundation of a people-based culture — respect, responsibility for problem identification and solving, and total integration into the methods of improvement. Without this foundation, initial gains from the application of tools will be temporary. Tools alone might provide brief symptomatic relief, but without new thinking based in a supportive culture, the tools do not support continuous improvement, and their use is not sustained. Ultimately, the use of lean tools without leadership-spurred cultural transformation appears doomed to fail.

Employees are Hickory Chair's "secret weapon." This is also the secret weapon that every business already has, and deployment does not require a search for either capital or new employees. What is required is the persistent, energetic, and disciplined pursuit of a new way of thinking grounded in ideals, values, a vision of the future, and good storytelling ability to unlock and use the skills of your existing employees.

"You've got to have faith in people. The creativity of our employees has been there all along," said Jay Reardon. "As we gained momentum with our improvement projects and recognized our employees' early successes, more of our employees have become involved and developed great ideas for even more improvements. Hundreds of little things are better than one home run. We see this as a continuing journey. As you achieve each new threshold, it gives you perspective about new opportunities."

> ## QUESTIONS
>
> - Do you have a business system or production system unique to your company?
> - Do your transformation efforts include organizational change?
> - Do your leaders seek help and information from outside sources? Are they genuinely committed to change?
> - Does your company provide training resources, including an in-house "university?"

Deborah Porto is the director, applied research, Industrial Extension Service, North Carolina State University in Waynesville, NC; she can be reached by email at deborah_porto@ncsu.edu.

Michael Smith, PhD is an assistant professor of management and international business at Western Carolina University in Cullowhee, NC; email at mesmith@wcu.edu.

REFERENCES

1. Womack, James P., Daniel T. Jones, and Daniel Roos, *The Machine that Changed the World*, Rawson Associates, New York, 1990.
2. Exemplars include: Dennis, Pascal, *Lean Production Simplified*, Productivity Press, New York, 2002; and Spear, Steven and H. Kent Bowen, "Decoding the DNA of the Toyota Production System," Harvard Business Review, September–October 1999.
3. Alder, Paul S., "Time-and-Motion Regained," Harvard Business Review, January–February 1993, pp. 97–108.
4. Ohno, Taiichi, *Toyota Production System Beyond Large Scale Production*, Productivity, Inc., Portland, OR, 1988.
5. Spear, Steven J., "Learning to Lead at Toyota," Harvard Business Review, May 2004, Vol. 82, Issue 5, pp. 78–86.
6. Liker, Jeffrey, *The Toyota Way: 14 Management Principles From The World's Greatest Manufacturer*, McGraw Hill, New York, 2004.

8

Stable Chaos: Leading Change in the Fast Lane

Douglas F. Carlberg

IN BRIEF

Stable chaos is maintaining stable, but highly flexible operations while constantly pursuing new initiatives to improve them. Being too chaotic is confusing; but some chaos is necessary for effective change. A veteran leader of an award-winning company tells his company story along with the method used to maintain stability amidst both planned and unplanned process changes.

"The big eat the small" used to be a common saying in the business world. But in today's environment, the fast eat the slow. With the pace of commerce increasing, companies unprepared to make changes quickly are likely to fall behind. Examples abound of yesterday's market leaders becoming today's also-rans. To remain competitive, it is essential to be both competent and quick at making effective changes in your business, and to implement processes that will facilitate significant, sustainable improvements.

M2 Global applies a battery of techniques to expedite improvements based on three enterprise building blocks: our technical, social, and communications systems. You can't change everything at once, so this keeps the business stable while making changes. We defined each of these macro-systems, ensuring that they are complementary; then subordinating all changes to these three systems. We've been on the road to excellence for 15 years, through lots of ups, downs, and distractions. We've used these macro-models to guide the day-to-day, tactical, and strategic needs of a small business, accumulating a number of lessons learned.

THE BIG PICTURE

How we arrived at our technical/social/communications macro-systems model requires further explanation. Early in our Total Quality journey we almost fell victim to theory-of-the-month fads. We learned two things pretty fast: You can create unhealthy chaos if you don't pay attention to what you are doing, and every new idea worth using requires intelligent adaptation for your business. While I believe in injecting some level of chaos to stimulate new thought (my staff's sometimes-affectionate nickname for me is "Captain Chaos"), you need to avoid wholesale disintegration of your business structures. And each new approach you try must be inserted in the context of your organization's values, culture, training, experience, reward system, etc.

Through a series of "ah-has!" we became aware of our own technical, social, and communications systems. They displayed a level of unconscious competence. We had a way of managing, doing, and measuring work: the technical system. We had a way of organizing, applying, and rewarding our people: the social system. And we had a way of communicating our successes and shortcomings: our common language of quality. At the time we were using manufacturing requirements planning with master scheduling for our factory (MRPII), had a healthy participative management style, and had invested heavily in training everyone per Philip Crosby's Quality Education System. It all worked pretty well at that moment. Then there was a new moment.

Total demand for production from the factory grew; low-volume/high-mix mass customization became the name of the game. To keep up with two shift's worth of problem solving, managers practically lived at the plant, on a stress curve to burnout. And although nonconformance to requirements was okay for measuring the cost of variability, customers expected something beyond meeting sales order specifications.

Had our model failed us? No, we just needed to recognize that we were responsible for more than its maintenance. We needed to guide its evolution as well.

If we were going to change one of the complementary systems it was likely to necessitate changes in the other two. With real pain to motivate us and some chaos injected for creative stimulus, my senior staff and

ABOUT M2 GLOBAL

M2 Global of San Antonio, TX is descended from a ferrite operation founded in 1958 by Bob Webb, an engineer and designer, who sold the business to Farinon Electric Company in 1977. In 1981, Harris Corporation, a $3 billion producer of high-technology communications and information processing equipment, purchased Farinon, naming it the Harris Farinon Division. In late 1999, Harris spun off this division to a group of its former managers and engineers, who formed M2 Global Technology Ltd. and M2 Global, Inc. Today it is a service-disabled-veteran-owned small business with annual revenues of approximately $8 million. M2 Global teams with two other small businesses to market defense services as Trilogy Defense Services.

M2 Global manufactures a broad range of complex microwave radio frequency (RF) components. Its ferrite isolators and circulators are industry leaders. It designs and manufactures high-performance wave-guides, couplers, dividers, and power splitters. In OEM customer equipment, its components reside in more than 100 countries in applications such as cell phone systems, satellite up-and-down links, radar systems, and high-definition TV broadcasting. M2 Global components are essential in Department of Defense equipment. In addition, M2 Global is a contract manufacturer specializing in prototypes and quick-turn production. To be in this business, quality is a must-have; versatility and short leadtimes are a competitive advantage.

Our microwave components are among the most reliable and sophisticated products commercially available, made to customer order from approximately 4000 base designs. Production is vertically integrated for quality control and short lead-times. M2 Global does it all: sheet metal fabrication, precision CNC machining, torch brazing, welding, heat treating, printed circuit board assembly, and more. Total production cycle time is ten calendar days; the best demonstrated total production cycle time to date is one day. Customer services include application engineering, rapid prototyping, and short cycle times for delivery and repair of discrepant field replaceable units. All this takes place in a new 25,000 square foot building with 80 employees. All departments are air conditioned, and two areas are clean rooms.

With this challenge, a cross-functional workforce is mandatory. Half of all operators can work on any process within M2 Global. Component and Fabrication team members have developed at least three operators certified to work every job in their area. Boundaries between exempt and non-exempt work blur. This versatility has been a major factor in both quality and productivity improvement in the past five years.

M2 Global is not shy about seeking certifications, awards, and outside learning. The operation has been ISO-9001 registered since 1994. It won a Shingo Prize in 1996. It is ISO-14001 compliant. It's been a finalist in Industry Week's Best Plants process. It was the 2006 Southwest Region winner of the AME Excellence Award. In July 2006, M2 Global attained AS9100 certification (described as a quality and safety standard "on steroids"). And it was one of the few companies accepted into the United States Air Force Manufacturing Technical Assistance Program.

I came to a series of decisions. The first was to tap the collective knowledge and wisdom of the workforce — this to free managers from day-to-day fire fighting. The second was to find a better manufacturing philosophy, one that had shorter total production times and required less materials on hand. Third ... well, the third decision was a long time coming because while making all the other changes, we could not afford to stop understanding each other, so the quality communication system stayed intact a while longer. I'll tell you about that at the end.

TEAM-BASED MANAGEMENT

Tapping into the strength of the workforce has been our most exciting and rewarding accomplishment. And creating it first was the singular thing that led to all the other successes. We set out to move from participative management to team based management. Separating *management* as a discipline from *manager* as a position has become the cornerstone of M2 Global's success in making rapid improvements. Combine that understanding with three guiding principles and you have a great start for bringing out the best in each other:

"The deepest desire in human nature is the desire to be great."

—Sigmund Freud

"Principle-centered leadership suggests that the highest level of human motivation is a sense of personal contribution."

—Stephen R. Covey

"Trust is the residual of promises kept."

—Colin Powell

With the evolution into team-based management for *all* business areas, internal on-time delivery percentages steadily increased to over 90 percent. The teams learned to manage and improve their own processes as well as their relationships with suppliers and customers. Monthly team reviews provide for goal deployment, measurement reporting, and corrective action if needed. New product introduction cycle time quickly dropped by 40 percent and keeps reducing. This allowed us to decrease the time between product upgrades from every three years to every two months.

For our transition to team-based management, we used a vehicle called Architecture For Excellence™ (from our days as a Harris division), which is a framework for high performance organizations. Our leadership teams have only two levels: the top Operations Leadership Team, and a set of linked functional leadership teams and Business Area Teams. Each Business Area Team aligns with a particular functional leadership team. Business Area Teams are semi-autonomous business units responsible for day-to-day operation of the business, plus identifying and implementing improvements within their unit. These teams are deployed throughout the business: manufacturing, materials, human resources, administration, finance and accounting, manufacturing support engineering, and information systems. Each team has only two primary objectives: to satisfy their customers and to improve their business. This improvement mission includes the growth and development of the team members themselves.

Developing teams to self-improve processes requires three levels of implementation: empowerment, enablement, and education. Empowerment gives team members some of the decision-making authority and responsibility formerly reserved for managers. Employees develop and implement their own solutions, keeping management informed rather than asking permission and waiting for review board approval. Now they make improvements almost immediately — which means there is no suggestion system. Results of their changes are reported during team reviews. Freedom to use your best judgment drives this approach.

Team enablement provides team members with the information needed (such as daily and annual operating plans) to make good decisions to help the company achieve its business goals. For instance, if workers know that shortages of certain parts are extending manufacturing cycle time, they can work on circumventing the problem (by ordering from a different supplier, etc.).

The education stage of the team process provides team members with the knowledge and training to fulfill their expanded roles. M2 Global's comprehensive training program has been critical to employees learning how to use increased company information to help the business achieve success. Training for each employee averages over 40 hours annually. The training department administers six major curricula: development, leadership, manufacturing, operations, quality, and safety. Courses include self-developed programs as well as those conducted by subject matter experts both inside and outside the company. The company provides liberal support for obtaining bachelors and graduate degrees.

The end result is a craftsman-like atmosphere of ownership of excellence. The principles of quality — and of customer satisfaction — are internalized rather than held externally as an institutional ideal. Workforce education and personal ownership of excellence have allowed M2 Global operations to achieve unprecedented flexibility and agility.

QUICK-RESPONSE MANUFACTURING

Team-based management took about a year to put in place. In the meantime, we decided to a make a major change in the technical system, shifting from the push approach of MRP to a pull approach. Instead of an order entering the front of the factory (that is, "push"), it would enter the back of the factory (that is, "pull"). Kanbans for every manufacturing Business Area Team were sized for enough parts or work in process (WIP) to support two weeks of demand — no more and no less. When kanbans are filled, a Business Area Team shifts its attention to its improvement efforts, which include measuring internal customer satisfaction. WIP management changed from a forecast to a consumption basis.

No doubt you can appreciate that supply-chain management is critical to this system. Without a constant supply of parts, a demand-based manufacturing system behaves like an engine starved for fuel. Material ordering has been simplified with barcodes and electronic commerce, and intensified with multiple orders being placed per day. Enterprise-integration links extend to customers and suppliers.

Given that the procurement leadtimes on some exotic materials are up to a year, it takes that long to fill all areas of the supply pipeline to preclude shortages. Of course, this requires constant updating of long-range sales forecasts and teaming agreements with key suppliers that provide free exchange of information. These supplier partnerships are based on a mutual sharing of business risk and reward.

This migration of the factory to quick-response manufacturing required dramatic increases in organizational effectiveness. One-up/one-down cross-training (and the concept of job roles rather than job descriptions) motivates team members to acquire additional job skills, and it helps relieve unplanned constraints in flow. The highly visual factory keeps employees informed of the status of activities and replenishment signals at all times. Team-based management mates well with just-in-time flow manufacturing.

And the outcomes? Total production cycle times have dropped from 45 days by default to ten days by design. These times are headed lower still with further improvements in test methods for our complex products. In addition, more rigorous criteria for design for manufacturing (DFM) and design for testing (DFT) are being incorporated into new products. Our goal is to make the total production cycle time an insignificant contributor to the total sales order cycle time, which in our business includes applications engineering, product environmental qualification, and testing.

FIGURE 8.1 Doug Carlberg talking with Jeffrey Lewis and Anabel Pepito in the Contract Manufacturing Area.

FIGURE 8.2 Efrain Reyes talking with Doug Carlberg in front of the CNC Mori Seiki in the Contract Manufacturing Area.

ADDITIONAL TOOLS

Thus far, I've described M2 Global using catch phrases such as supplier partnership, bar code, electronic commerce, cross-training, kanban, and visual factory. Note that all these were in the context of the technical and social systems. They are just tools used within the macro business systems.

Several additional tools we've applied are worth mentioning:

- Process characterization is done by the Leadership Team and every Business Area Team to identify suppliers, customers, and processes that produce products and services — and key measures. This links each team to business goal deployment, and becomes the baseline for improvement and change management.
- 5S training for assessing and improving workplace organization for efficiency is delivered only to entire teams. (5S is derived from five Japanese words with rough equivalents in English: sort (organization), set in order (orderliness), shine (cleanliness), standardize (standardized cleanup), and sustain (discipline). An actual 5S event launches a team's competencies to apply these principles in their own work areas.
- Visual Systems concepts are being deployed to further link the teams' awareness with the technical system's status.
- Most internally-developed training avoids lecture in favor of heuristic approaches based on the Socratic Method. This method facilitates adult learning and is a perfect match to our team-based management system. It requires direct involvement of the participants, not just their attendance.
- *Kaizen* (the Japanese term for continuous improvement) is a disciplined approach to making effective process changes. Traditionally, it entails many incremental improvements over an extended period of time, eventually adding up to a significant impact. *The Kaizen Blitz* (named by AME) is an accelerated version of kaizen designed to produce dramatic results in just one week. Changes must be sustainable, so that the improvements continue over time. M2 Global's kaizen champions must qualify the goals within a strategic context to preclude random acts of improvement, which limits the chance of sub-optimization. But the executing team picks how goals are to

be achieved and negotiates self-imposed measurements — typically either halving or doubling a measure, depending on which direction is desirable. Consequently our kaizen teams adopt improvement "contracts" rather than having "mandates."

- Our plant uses computer-integrated manufacturing (CIM) technologies for rapid prototyping, improved documentation, and greater consistency in manufacturing process. CIM also is used in applications such as direct download of assembly bills of material and to link engineering's computer assisted design (CAD) system to automated assembly machines. Cycle time is decreased by drastic reduction of data entry time and by eliminating keying errors and resultant assembly errors. Personal computers automate assembly and test operations. An automated call distribution system has increased customer calls answered in person from 78 percent to over 90 percent.

- Business systems modules link engineering, manufacturing, and customer service via a local area network/wide area network for in-process production communications. Additionally, a Corrective Action Request and Corrective Action Tracking System links all business functions.

THE RESULTS

Indicators such as those in Figure 8.3 tell us that we're making progress, but are not yet close to perfection — and that we arm-wrestle technically demanding issues. But they do not show the most important aspect of M2 Global's journey. Our initiatives have created more than flexibility and agility — we call it adaptability. Our concept of enterprise integration is based on our macro-models. These, with the core practice at the heart of each one, are: 1) social (team-based management), 2) technical (just-in-time flow manufacturing), and 3) communication (a common language of quality, such as DMAIC, etc.). To preserve stability and operational integrity, all other concepts, including new tools and changes, are subordinated to this model. Adhering to this basic philosophy has helped the company achieve a customer satisfaction ranking of number one among its North American competitors.

FIRE IN THE PLANT: A MAJOR DISTRACTION

On July 8, 2005, a heater set a PVC ventilating hood on fire. Officially the fire was considered minor, confined to one area and quickly extinguished. But thick, acrid smoke wafted through the building, creating havoc with high-precision machines, tooling, and test equipment. A contaminated clean room is no trivial mess. Without the advantage of M2 Global's operational flexibility, the damage could have forced the company to close.

M2 Global followed the script of a disaster recovery plan that had last been updated when the Y2K millennium bug buzzed through business. Although a fire is a far different kind of peril, the plan worked well. Nonetheless, the 90 days after the fire were days of 24/7 work and intense adaptation.

First, we were delayed from re-entering the building until the fire marshal established an official cause. Once we were back in, most of the machines had (at the very least) to be disassembled and cleaned, and one had to be replaced. Cleaning up the programmable controllers alone cost $40,000. Equipment supplier technicians had to inspect most of the equipment before it could be used again. Very little of this work was a simple "wipe down" job.

M2 Global prioritized customer orders. Which ones were urgently needed by customers? Which could be delayed? Based on that assessment, we outsourced work. We moved restored machines to uncontaminated areas to resume work. Personnel figured out alternative ways to perform some processes. Plant activity returned to about 80 percent within a week, and we did not lose any customers.

After 90 days M2 Global had largely returned to normal, but normal did not last long. The landlord of the building refused to renew the lease. We began to look for new quarters, and found a building that could be modified to our purposes, moving in less than a year after the fire. On June 21, 2006 M2 Global held an open house to celebrate our return to more routine episodes of constructive chaos.

M2 Global Process Improvement by Some Key Indicators, 2003–2006

	2003	2004	2005	2006
Scrap as a % of Cost of Goods	0.61%	2.67%	0.52%	0.57%
Internal Nonconforming Quality Costs	1.21%	2.63%	1.62%	1.04%
Contract Mfg. Scrap, % of Cost of Goods	0.53%	0.80%	0.33%	0.00%
Development Cost per Part (Dollars)	3800	1200	900	700
On-time Delivery	86.5%	92.0%	86.6%	91.3%

FIGURE 8.3

We've long understood that making changes in business is a lot like changing a tire on a car while it is going 70 miles an hour. Unlike engineering, there is no experimental control sample for business process change — most changes we make are an act of faith. So as a sanity check, we also engage in "Olympic" benchmarking to absolute standards of excellence by subjecting ourselves to the scrutiny of several local and national organizations.

WHAT'S NEXT?

I deferred revealing a decision to change our common language of quality. Only recently have we decided to embrace an adaptation of quality function deployment (QFD). This is being applied to both our internal and external customers to close any perceived gaps between basic conformance to requirements and unmet, and perhaps previously unexpressed, expectations. We have also initiated training in Lean Six Sigma concepts to better understand the margin of our successes and the variability of our less successful endeavors. With our foundation in Phil Crosby's quality education concepts, these are not difficult conceptually, but they are expected to significantly improve our ability to bring next-level solutions to our customers and to evaluate our success in doing so.

Every day is a great adventure conducting business in today's global markets— little about them is predictable. A saying I once heard (but don't know the source) stays constantly in my mind: "Change is inevitable … Growth is optional." While that describes the challenge, a quote from that great American humorist Will Rogers guides our direction: "Even if you're on the right track, you can get run over if you don't keep moving."

QUESTIONS

- Do you tap the collective knowledge and wisdom of your workforce?
- Do you develop teams through empowerment, enablement and education?
- Is your production based on a pull approach or a push system?
- Is your organization flexible and agile?

Douglas F. Carlberg is president of M2 Global Technology Ltd., and president of AME's Southwest Region. He can be reached at 210/561–4800, or email at dcarlberg@m2global.com.

9

How Human Resource Departments Can Help Lean Transformation

Dr. Monica W. Tracey and Jamie W. Flinchbaugh

IN BRIEF

Many anecdotes from practitioner experience attest that the human side of lean is the hardest. While the authors' survey statistically confirmed much of this wisdom, it also revealed a few surprises. Their conclusion is that to sustain lean operations, the human resources function must support them, beginning with hiring people who are likely to be happy and to succeed in a lean working culture.

Companies have begun to understand that lean is about more than 5-S and U-shaped cells. It is also about people, culture, and leadership. However, Human Resource (HR) departments seldom seem to take an active role in lean transformations. How can companies and their HR departments better engage the full human potential of lean? To assist answering this question, we conducted a research study. From it, we discovered from actual practice not only how HR, but leadership creates better organizational conditions to support lean transformation.

Our results indicated that five key variables predict successful lean transformation:

1. Development of teams as a supporting structure of lean
2. Calculation and communication of metrics
3. Communication among organization members, particularly across organizational barriers
4. Communication to employees regarding their specific role in lean transformation
5. Acknowledgement and celebration of successes toward lean transformation.

Our research indicates that these are areas in which dramatic change in HR departments can accelerate a successful lean transformation.

But first, a note on the general state of HR in the context of leading change. HR departments have taken the brunt of punishment for inability to effectively engage employees in change programs. For example, the August 2005 cover page article in *Fast Company* magazine is titled, "Why We Hate HR." Everyone gets a laugh from Scott Adams' Dilbert cartoons portraying Catbert, the evil HR director, but laughs don't solve the problem.

Adopting lean principles well beyond core manufacturing has dramatically changed many other corporate internal functions, including product development, supply chain management, and more recently, accounting. But in too many companies, HR remains untouched by their company's commitment to lean. And for those who have engaged HR to help with lean transformation, the contribution has not reached its potential.

STEPS IN OUR RESEARCH OF LEAN

Before designing our survey, we completed an extensive literature review of existing research, to identify variables and factors relating to instituting a lean transformation. From this review, six areas seemed of particular importance to investigate further by administering a survey:

- Demographics (age, sex, ethnicity, etc.)
- Work Environment
- Innovation, Tools, and Technology
- Lean Implementation
- Communication
- Rewards/Benefits of Lean Implementation

We designed two separate surveys: One addressed employees working under direct supervision; the other addressed supervisors and managers charged with ensuring lean practices within their department(s). Each survey asked similar general questions, but different role-specific questions related to the implementation of lean.

Survey questions were written and grouped into one of the six categories derived from our literature review. Sixty-four questions were on the employee survey; 66 questions — two more — on the manager survey. Both questionnaires required ten to 15 minutes to complete.

After the survey design was completed and reviewed by the researchers, it was reviewed by two subject matter experts who had extensive experience with lean transformations, and who serve on the Pawley Institute board of directors. Both subject matter experts recommended changes to the content and wording of the survey instrument. After these modifications, the questionnaire was uploaded into a website entitled surveymonkey.com, which compiled the data as it was collected by those visiting the site to take the survey.

Survey respondents were from corporations recruited through local manufacturing membership associations, or who were involved with The Pawley Institute. Both electronic and written communications encouraged people from these sites to complete the survey by using the website, mail, or visits from the researchers if desired. The majority of those completing the questionnaire used the surveymonkey.com website. Corporations who did not provide website access to all survey participants distributed hard copies of the survey amongst their employee population.

Survey data was captured from respondents in 72 different sites or companies; 154 workers completed the employee survey; and 72 managers completed the management survey. The percentage of persons who had seen the survey prior to responding is unknown, but all persons who did respond completed every question on the survey. Only the conclusions from the survey are reported here; the statistical analysis is omitted.

GENERAL RESEARCH FINDINGS AND DISCUSSION

Our research results demonstrated that, despite the significant history of lean and its application within companies of all types and sizes, documentation of conditions for success is generally elusive. Lean transformation may be one of the most powerful means to improve businesses, but far too few companies achieve the promised gains. From the view of the research, five key variables predicted the perception, at least, of successful lean implementation. The following findings and conclusions relate each of these five key variables to the engagement of HR implementing lean.

1. Development of teams as a supporting structure

Teams are an important element of a lean organization. We believe, and the research supports, that the development of effective teams extends deep both inside and outside of lean transformations. Within lean, teams are important because the whole process must work together to build value for the customer, and if teams cannot work together then the process cannot work for the customer. How teams work is more important than their mere existence.

Teams in a lean environment need the following: first, a common language, common principles, and common tools. Second, a common drive provided by vision, metrics, and goals. Third, they need to design the work around them visually so that there is high agreement about what work must be done and how it should be done — and immediately exposing problems so that they may be resolved.

No surprise so far, but fourth, and perhaps most important, teams need both the capability and the skills to manage themselves. In a lean environment, teams need a great deal of autonomy to manage and improve their process, but this is not done in a vacuum. Teams are still part of the larger organization around them. Providing more autonomy than necessary before maturity can be a big mistake, for with this new authority comes new responsibility — the responsibility to function as a productive team together — and with other teams.

2. Calculation and communication of metrics

Metrics keep score and determine if progress is being made. In a lean environment, we found that several criteria should be considered when developing metric systems or scoreboards. First, a scoreboard and its relevant metrics must be "owned" by those who own the process, whether a cell team on the floor, or an office team such as customer service. Therefore, metrics must be easy to update by these process owners. Second, metrics must be as predictive as possible, with only a small fraction of the metrics looking rearward. Because these metrics should support daily decision making, predictive metrics offer much more useful decision support than those that are rearward facing. Third, management must support the metrics; they must decide who will review the metrics, when they will do so, what they will look for, and how will they respond to the metrics with action. Fourth, and perhaps most importantly, the metrics must point in a steady and consistent direction toward the ideal state.

3. Communication across boundaries

Companies that are successful in lean are also successful improving their communications, particularly across boundaries such as departments and functions. Although understandable, this was one of our more surprising research findings. In a lean environment, process focus takes priority over functional focus. Successful lean processes have material or information flowing across functional boundaries, so naturally companies that are successful in lean will also improve communications across functional boundaries in the manner most efficient and effective for the customer.

The research found that communication in a lean environment must be vertical, horizontal — and two-way. It is not enough for a lean leader to be excellent communicating the vision and direction to the masses of the organization; he must also convey information about the changes going on at the top. Lean changes both the work and the way people think, so employees need to see that individuals at the top of the organization are changing the way they think before they will do the same.

Bottom-up communication is equally important. It provides valuable, timely information about changes that are going on, and about new barriers that arise as progress is made.

Horizontal communication must occur, not up-across-down, but directly from the source of the information to the need. The ability to communicate, and for that communication to be received and used, is important to assure process experimentation where the work is done. Increased experimentation can result either in increased chaos or in organization-wide improvement. The key variable differentiating between these two states is how well an organization communicates directly from person to person.

4. Communication to employees regarding their role

Part of management's communication for lean implementation includes clarity of each employee's roles and responsibilities. This communication, however, is a two-person process. Lack of employee commitment was found to be one of the top barriers to implementing continuous improvement. This study traced the roots of employees' negative attitudes to the management team not consistently communicating with them. In addition, it was discovered that employees need to be trained in communication and discussion techniques; otherwise they really do not understand how to ask questions and how to elicit feedback.

When many companies begin their lean journeys, they train everyone in lean — then give everyone the same role: Go out and apply lean. However, as with any other aspect of an organization, success depends upon role clarity. Roles must change as an organization goes toward lean maturity, so the rate at which an organization reaches maturity partly depends on lean role clarity and integration throughout the journey. Maintaining role clarity as these roles dramatically change appears to be an important criterion of success.

5. Acknowledgment and celebrations of successes

Most corporate initiatives have a distinct beginning and a clear, objective outcome, but lean is a never-ending journey. If objectives remain clear, employees at all levels can feel a sense of accomplishment and if appropriate, the accompanying reward. But since lean is an endless journey, employees are unsure when to celebrate accomplishment. Simultaneously celebrating and raising awareness of the remaining performance gap is a tough balancing act. However, this research demonstrated that companies that find ways to celebrate success along the journey are more successful at lean. They clearly define milestones, communicate progress toward them, and celebrate successes along the journey.

So how does an organization acknowledge success on a never-ending journey? First, they must learn to recognize and communicate progress. Then they must decide how to reward such progress, if at all.

Recognizing success in lean first requires that it be understood as a journey. Without implying that ultimate lean has been achieved, leadership must balance recognition of the success achieved with maintaining the tension for future progress. If tension is sustained without recognizing progress, organization-wide burnout will follow. Managers should understand that what they choose to recognize as success, and how they choose to recognize it, can either reinforce human progress or retard it.

Rewarding progress is an even more complicated challenge. All solutions to the reward problem have downsides. Some of them can be catastrophic. Suppose you reward people in proportion to the size of the ideas they contribute; all you will get are big ideas, and you will minimize the development of people not in position to make big contributions. Another big problem is that rewards can quickly become entitlements, losing the intended affect. Some of the most successful organizations give no significant direct compensation for ideas contributed or for participation in lean. Unfortunately, we know of no thorough empirical data supporting a commonsense lean practice: that the most effective encouragement is to support the people contributing ideas day-in and day-out by listening to those ideas and acting upon them.

RECOMMENDATIONS FOR HR DEPARTMENTS

If you are an HR manager, or connected to an HR department, what steps can we recommend that you take, based on this survey? General recommendations must be framed as "areas HR should enroll themselves in." Specific solutions that emerge will vary depending on the company, its history, and its challenges.

Culture: Creating a lean culture is to create an environment that supports four of the five predictors from this study: 1) teams developed and functioning to support the structure of lean, 2) communication processes that operate across boundaries, 3) clarity of all employees' roles in the lean organization, and 4) a process for calculating and communicating metrics is in place and followed by process owners.

Future research on how to create and maintain such a culture is needed, including defining more specifically the artifacts and beliefs of that lean culture.

Recruitment Seeking the Character Traits Needed: Ability to communicate, work in teams, create and follow measurements, work across organizational boundaries, and identify and celebrate successes. If these traits are present in some form in employees implementing lean, they may be enhanced. But if not basically present, they may not be able to be taught (Collins, 2001). Therefore, the recruitment and hiring process should identify and select these traits.

Future research on how to recruit and hire a lean-ready person is needed. This includes the criteria and methods to predict leaders of lean, as well as those which would fail in a lean environment.

Pay/Recognition and Performance Structure: The fifth predictor in this study identified the importance of rewards and recognition and the acknowledgement and celebrations of success. A fair and suitable reward and recognition program is vital in the recruitment and retention of employees, especially in a lean implementation process. This does not imply a high pay structure, but rather considered fair and equitable. Just as studies have shown that executives who were successful in creating great companies were not necessarily the highest paid (Collins, 2001), the same thing may apply to others.

Future research on how to pay and reward a lean employee is needed, and what levers beyond pay most contribute to lean success.

Developing, Choosing, and Maintaining Lean Leaders: Leadership in a lean environment can quickly be distinguished from traditional views on leadership. Lean is a long-term, evolutionary, and inclusive environment. Leadership for it differs from crisis-based, charge-the-hill hero leadership. Understanding the choice between developing leadership for lean and choosing leaders who would support lean must be examined and methods examined. We need to further explore the skills and capabilities to maintain leadership over a long period of time (Spear, 2004), and the conflict between long tenure and high demand for such individuals in the external job market.

NEXT STEPS IN FORMAL RESEARCH

Boyer (1996) states that the determinants of lean production system success are the actions taken, the principles implemented, and the changes made to the organization to achieve the desired performance. This research supports Boyer's premise along with the critical finding that the predictors of lean success are neither unique, nor specific to manufacturing. That is, respondents did not choose lean tools as a contributor to lean success. Rather, all five primary predictors are "human" issues, and those are the domain, although not exclusively, of HR departments. Yet the literature is limited on how HR supports and enables lean implementation as supported.

Future research in how human resources enables lean must address these predictors, which in turn should increase lean transformation success. Lean in human resources must be distinguished from HR-enabled lean. Lean in human resources is defined as driving waste out of HR processes. HR-enabled lean is how the human-resource processes and functions help create lean success throughout the organization.

This research should drive deeper into the predictors of lean success. Several key questions will be explored for each of the five predictors, such as:

1. Why is it a predictor of lean success?
2. What are the best practices within this predictor?
3. What factors should be avoided in this predictor?
4. How can HR organizations provide value in support of this predictor?

We plan to extend this research, and as always, participation and funding is required. If you would like to participate in the future phases of this research, please contact us.

QUESTIONS

- Is your HR department involved in your lean transformation?
- Does your recruitment process include a focus on the skills and characteristics desired in lean employees? In lean leaders?
- Does your HR department strive for two-way communication with employees?
- Do you provide compensation and incentives consistent with a lean workplace?

Monica W. Tracey is assistant professor in the Human Resource Development Department at Oakland University, Rochester, MI and a founding member of the Pawley Institute: tracey@oakland.edu.

Jamie Flinchbaugh is co-founder and partner of the Lean Learning Center in Novi, MI and is co-author of *The Hitchhiker's Guide to Lean: Lessons from the Road*: jamie@leanlearningcenter.com

REFERENCES

Boyer, K.K., "An assessment of managerial commitment to lean production," International Journal of Operations & Production Management Vol. 19, No. 9, 1996, pp. 48–59.

Collins, J., *Good to Great: Why Some Companies Make the Leap and Others Don't*, Harper Collins Publishing, New York, NY, 2001.

Hammonds, Keith H., "Why we hate HR," Fast Company, August, 2005, pp. 40–47.

Spear, Steven J., "Learning to Lead at Toyota," Harvard Business Review, No. R0405E, May, 2004, pp. 78–86.

Index